The Lessons of Experience

How Successful Executives Develop on the Job

Morgan W. McCall, Jr.
Michael M. Lombardo
Ann M. Morrison

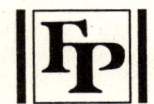

THE FREE PRESS
New York   London   Toronto   Sydney

Copyright © 1988 by Lexington Books

All rights reserved. No part of this book may be reproduced or transmitted in any form or by any means, electronic or mechanical, including photocopying, recording, or by any information storage and retrieval system, without permission in writing from the Publisher.

The Free Press
A Division of Simon & Schuster Inc.
1230 Avenue of the Americas
New York, N.Y. 10020

Printed in the United States of America

printing number
31 33 35 37 39 40 38 36 34 32

Library of Congress Cataloging-in-Publication Data

McCall, Morgan W.
   The lessons of experience.

(The Issues in organization and management series)
   Bibliography: p.
   Includes index.
   1. Executive ability. 2. Executives. 3. Experiential learning.   I. Lombardo, Michael M. II. Morrison, Ann M. III. Title. IV. Series.
HD38.2.M393   1988   658.4′09   87-46405
         ISBN-13: 978-0-669-18095-4
         ISBN-10:   0-669-18095-5

*To Morgan III and Brent,
in hopes that their
experiences will treat them kindly;
to Ginny and Esther,
who helped us live through this experience;
and to Reba and Dinny, with love and thanks*

Contents

Figures   vii

Foreword   ix
Warren Bennis

Acknowledgments   xi

1. Developing Executive Talent   1

2. Trial by Fire: Learning from Job Assignments   15

3. When Other People Matter   67

4. Hardships   87

5. Making the Most of Experience   121

6. Making It Work: The Corporate Opportunity   147

Appendix: The Original Interview Guide   189

Notes   195

References   201

Index   205

About the Authors   209

Figures

1-1. The Development of Effective General Managers   4
1-2. The Potential Lessons of Experience   7
1-3. The Developmental Events   10
2-1. The Potential Lessons of Early Work Experience   25-26
2-2. The Potential Lessons of First Supervisory Experience   30-31
2-3. The Potential Lessons of Project and Task Force Assignments   36-37
2-4. The Potential Lessons of Line-to-Staff Switches   40-41
2-5. The Potential Lessons of Starting from Scratch   46-47
2-6. The Potential Lessons of Fix-Its   52-53
2-7. The Potential Lessons of Scope   56-57
2-8. Potential Learning from Assignments   61
2-9. The Potential Lessons of Assignments   62
3-1. The Potential Lessons of Other People   84-85
4-1. The Potential Lessons of Personal Traumas   94-95
4-2. The Potential Lessons of a Career Setback   100-101
4-3. The Potential Lessons of Changing Jobs   105-106
4-4. The Potential Lessons of Business Failures and Mistakes   112-113
4-5. The Potential Lessons of Subordinate Performance Problems   115-116
4-6. Learning from Hardships   117

4-7. The Potential Lessons of Hardships   118–119
5-1. A Framework for Development   139
5-2. Balance   145
6-1. Corporation or Conglomerate?   150
6-2. Some Pros and Cons of a Strong Foundation for Development   159–160
6-3. Checklist for Identifying Developmental Jobs   163
6-4. The Ten Fatal Flaws   168–169
6-5. Checklist for Creating a Talent Pool   170
6-6. Checklist for Breadth versus Depth Issues   171
6-7. Checklist for Responsibility for Development   174
6-8. Checklist for Helping People Learn from Experience   180
6-9. Checklist for Coursework and Training   183

Foreword

In the last several decades, a flood of books on management has hit American bookstores, perhaps in response to what *Time* magazine recently called "the leadership crisis." Unfortunately, too many of these books reduce what is, in fact, an endless process to quick fixes and formulas: Just say the magic word and you, too, can become an effective executive. Happily, *The Lessons of Experience* not only gives the lie to such simplistic nonsense but also describes the nuts and bolts mechanics of managerial development in great detail.

Recognizing from the outset that good management is more an art than a science and that superior executives are made, not born, and, for the most part, self-made, the authors get right down to business. *The Lessons of Experience* is just that, as it is based on the actual experiences of hundreds of managers around the country, as limned in several studies. This is not theory; this is fact—communiques from the trenches of corporate America. The good news is that our best and brightest are as smart, innovative, and capable as any generation of executives has ever been. The bad news, in this era of instant gratification, is that the route to the top is as arduous and tricky as it has ever been. Indeed, the authors have devoted an entire chapter to "hardships."

There is perhaps no better definition of the process than Jacob Bronowski's, as cited by the authors: "We have to understand that the world can only be grasped by action, not by contemplation. . . . The most powerful drive in the ascent of man is his pleasure in his own skill. He loves to do what he does well and, having done it well, he loves to do it better."

The executives the authors describe and quote are people of action, people who regard everything—from bad bosses to crises to triumphs—as an opportunity to learn, who have not only developed their strengths but also compensated for their weaknesses, who have recognized early that in contemporary corporate culture there is no such thing as a successful one-man band, and who have, above all, relished the doing.

It has been my own experience that the one quality, aside from built-in gifts, which separates the extraordinary executives from the ordinary is the pleasure they take in their work. Such people are not fueled by some simplistic ambition but by what I have come to think of as a passion for the promises of life. This passion manifests itself in everything they do—from dealing with difficult bosses to building a new overseas plant from scratch.

Aside from its impressive array of data, its refreshingly candid and clear language, and its wealth of practical advice, the principal merit of *The Lessons of Experience* is its gut truth: The primary responsibility for effective management development resides in the managers themselves. There are many things a corporation can do, as the authors note, to encourage its talented executives, but only if the talent is there and willing and able to develop itself.

The authors do not claim that the process is easy or quick. Indeed, they take the opposite position: It is hard and, often, slow, and there are many risks and pitfalls along the way, as many opportunities to fail as to succeed. But I know of no book which more accurately describes the pleasures as well as the pain of the process.

In this sense, *The Lessons of Experience* is unique. It restores the romance inherent in the business of business by, of all things, looking at it realistically.

Warren Bennis

Acknowledgments

This book was written for a general audience and therefore contains little technical detail. But beneath it lies a foundation of five years of empirical work, numerous efforts to apply the findings, and countless sessions with executives and managers. Cecil B. DeMille would have admired the cast of thousands who, in one way or another, contributed to this manuscript. First and foremost are the nearly two hundred managers and executives who recounted their experiences to us in the various studies. This book is literally theirs, for it tells their stories. No less important are the hundreds of additional managers and executives who, in discussions, other studies, presentations, seminars, and workshops, helped us to interpret what we had learned and to draw from it implications for developing executive talent. Our greatest hope is that we have done justice to their collective wisdom, and our deepest regret is that we can't list each of them by name.

Second only to the executives who provided the information is our colleague at the Center for Creative Leadership, Bill Drath, who invested countless hours as editor, critic, cajoler, jester, negotiator, cheerleader, sounding board, and friend.

The magnitude of this undertaking is reflected not only in the large number of executives and managers involved but also in the small army of individuals who worked with us in gaining access to corporations, collecting and analyzing data, funding the efforts, and disseminating the results. Expressions of gratitude must start with four individuals who, in 1981, worked with us to determine exactly what we would study and then persuaded their corporations to support it. Sara Clope and Steve Wall were the first two to chance collaboration, followed shortly by Bill Saunders and Jim Thurber. Without them, the project would never have left the flip chart.

Our first two studies involved intensive, lengthy interviews with 105 executives in which we were assisted by Bob Kaplan and Anne Faber, and which produced intimidating quantities of notes waiting for analysis. Joining us initially in this task was Randy White, whose first day at the Center introduced him to a stack of interview notes taller than he was. Shortly afterward, Esther Lindsey joined the fray, and later Joan Kofodimos. Somehow among us we made sense of the initial data and set the stage for the bulk of the research yet to do.

A new team of McCall, Lombardo, Lindsey, and White, in various combinations and roles, proceeded to study top executives in three additional large corporations. Each study substantially enlarged our initial findings—and the number of people who helped us out. As we progressed, we were joined by three new corporate collaborators—Mike Burns, Don Canning, and Bob Eichinger—who opened doors and worked with us to make sense of the results. Gargantuan coding sessions drew on the additional skills of Betty Ann Bailey and Ginny Homes. As the sample sizes grew larger, we enlisted the aid of Phil Bobko and Mark Applebaum as statistical consultants, and Saralyn Griffith, who analyzed the data. Additional studies formed, and Cindy McCauley, Marian Ruderman, and Claire Usher joined in the project. All of this effort resulted in a detailed technical book documenting the results of the studies and forming the backbone of this volume (Esther Lindsey, Virginia Homes, and Morgan McCall, *Key Events in Executives' Lives,* Greensboro, N.C.: Center for Creative Leadership, 1987).

At long last came the arduous task of putting the manuscript together. Many of our professional colleagues provided helpful feedback on seemingly endless drafts and redrafts. At the Center these included David DeVries, Bill Drath, Bob Kaplan, Esther Lindsey, and Randy White. Outside we imposed upon Warren

Acknowledgments

Bennis, Gene Cattabiani, Miriam Clark, Bob Eichinger, Jack Gabarro, Larry Kahn, Allen Kraut, Paula Litchfield, Joel Moses, Toni Ondrasik, and Jay Thompson. Berkeley Rice helped with restructuring parts of the book and put together some of the sections on early work experiences. Gene Cattabiani and Jim Roberts allowed us to interview them extensively on tape for additional detail. Last but not least are Bob Bovenshulte, general manager of Lexington Books, and series editors Ben Schneider and Art Brief, whose faith as well as feedback were instrumental. We are immensely grateful to all of them for their helpfulness, kind words, and constructive comments.

Perhaps the toughest task of all remained to our absolutely first-rate support staff, spearheaded by Tracy Dobbins, who was ably assisted by Marcia Horowitz and Linda Ravel. Thanks, too, to Patty Ohlott, who helped us track down and keep track of the footnotes and references. Help with earlier drafts of the manuscript came from Cynthia Anthony, Martha Bennett, Tina Culp, Kris Dyson, Teri Hunter, Jeanese Joyner, B. J. Moore, Cindy Norris, and Ellen Ramsey.

We thank you all. Without you this couldn't have happened, and we hope you share our pride in this book. A project like this isn't cheap, and was only possible through the sustained support of our current and past corporate sponsors during the years of the project—Sun Company, Union Carbide Corporation, Westinghouse Electric, and Armco (our four charter members) and American Express, General Electric, Goodyear Tire and Rubber, Merrill Lynch, Nabisco Brands, PepsiCo, and Pillsbury—and of the Center for Creative Leadership. This work has been enriched through the active collaboration of the corporate representatives who have struggled with us (and, perhaps even more significantly, been patient with us). Special thanks to Gene Andrews, Jesse Blackman, Kent Bradshaw, Mike Burns, John Butler, Joel DeLuca, Bob Eichinger, Bruce Franklin, Glenn Jeffries, Geri Kurlander, Jay Thompson, and Ron Trowbridge. Together we have proven that collaboration between researchers and practitioners, while seldom easy, can work.

I'm sittin' and rockin' in front of the fire
Thinkin' of things as they are
And how all that I am is just pieces and parts
Of the memories I've gathered so far.
Here's to the goodness and kindness I've shown
Here's to the people that I've treated wrong
Here's to mistakes that I wish I could change
Here's to the pride and the shame
And the growin' that comes with the pain.

I'm sittin' and rockin' in front of the fire
Thinkin' of things yet to be
How the present's a doorway that leads from the past
To a future that I've yet to see.
Here's to the man that I was in the past
Here's to the man that I am now at last
Here's to the man that I someday will be
Here's hopin' he's better than me
Because of these old memories.
—Mike Cross
Rock'n'Rye
© 1980 Vic-Ray Publishing
(ASCAP)

From the album "Mike Cross—Rock'n'Rye" (Sugar Hill Records—SH/GR-1004). Reprinted with permission.

1
Developing Executive Talent

If you ask senior executives how much their corporations invest in management development, you may hear about the size of their human resource budget, the cost of the new education center, how many people were sent to Harvard last year, the number of full-time training staff employed, or the number of courses listed in the corporate course catalog. Estimating the annual investment in the corporate classroom is no small feat, but two different sources place it in the range of $40 billion.[1]

This figure would be impressive under any circumstances, but it is only a small portion of the actual investment in development. Only a minute part of a manager's time is spent in the classroom, suggesting that it's in the other 99.9 percent of the time that the bulk of development takes place. In other words, people develop on the job, and the expenses associated with learning-while-doing are part of the investment in development. To even approach the *actual* investment in management development, one would have to consider the costs associated with developmentally driven changes in job assignments. Relocation expenses, salary increases, losses in efficiency and errors during the learning process, and the cost of failure in a new assignment could all be viewed as part of the investment in development. One company estimated, for example, that a failed general manager costs $500,000, not counting the negative impact on business revenue.[2]

If one considers both the classroom and the job, then the investment in development is astronomical. If it routinely produced effective managers and executives, it would be money well spent, and that would be the end of it. But, unfortunately, the return on this investment is anything but clear. Classroom activities as developmental interventions are more tangible than on-the-job experiences and, while difficult to assess, have received considerable research attention. To say that the results have been equivocal is a generous interpretation. Investing in the corporate classroom for management development remains more an act of faith than an empirically justified activity.

But if the impact of the classroom is uncertain, the impact of on-the-job management development is virtually unexplored. We know that job challenge is crucial to development of managerial abilities,[3] and we know that reputedly better managed firms make extensive use of work experiences for development,[4] but our knowledge of what experiences matter, why they matter, and what people get out of them is skimpy at best. In a recent report on this topic, McCauley[5] found that her "review of the empirical literature revealed no systematic body of research focused on what experiences or events may be important in managers' careers."

Leaders: Born or Made?

The fact that we are talking about tens (and perhaps hundreds) of billions of dollars invested in developmental activities is sufficient grounds for scrutinizing practices, but an examination of development begins with assumptions about the nature of human—and especially adult—development.

Some executives we have worked with maintain that leadership is not something that can be trained or developed. You have it or you don't. Other executives act as if any clay can be pounded or formed into an effective manager. The ultimate in egalitarianism, their assumption is that all of us are potential leaders if only the proper education or experience could be found to release those abilities.

As heated and entertaining as the nature/nurture debates can be, they seriously distract us from getting on with the business of development. While the research can never be definitive, sufficient evidence exists to conclude that neither explanation is adequate. There is no longer any question that some predisposing factors are primarily genetic,[6] or at least developed so early in life that they cannot be changed much in later years. Basic intellectual capacity, for example, appears to be in one's wiring.[7]

Another chunk of predisposing characteristics, if not genetic, seems to be the product of growing up—the socialization of the pre-work years. The lessons of life's experiences begin early, with the influence of family, peers, education, sports, and other events of childhood shaping the manager-to-be.

When it comes to managerial and executive effectiveness, it is not possible to provide a comprehensive list of all potentially relevant characteristics and the ages at which they are acquired. John Kotter, in his study of corporate general managers,[8] suggested one possible scenario, partially reproduced in figure 1–1. He concluded that the general managers he studied had some background experiences in common, which in turn resulted in common characteristics such as optimism, emotional stability, and desire for achievement and power.

Volumes have been devoted to efforts at predicting executive effectiveness by measuring personality traits, cognitive abilities, and background experiences, all to modest avail.[9] Even the most sophisticated and expensive assessment technique, the assessment center, usually can account for only 10 to 20 percent of the variability in managerial promotion rates.[10] More important than the modest associations between these endless lists of variables and the various criteria of performance is the unassailable fact that senior executives do not emerge full blown. Whatever genetic endowment, whatever home life, however good the education, a future executive does not walk into a corporation knowing how to sell steam turbine generators to the Chinese.

So the issue is that people who emerge as candidates for executive jobs may come with a lot of givens, but what happens to them on the job matters. Knowledge of how the business works, ability to work with senior executives, learning to manage people who were once peers, negotiating with hostile foreign governments, handling tense political situations, firing people—these and many others are the lessons of experience. They are

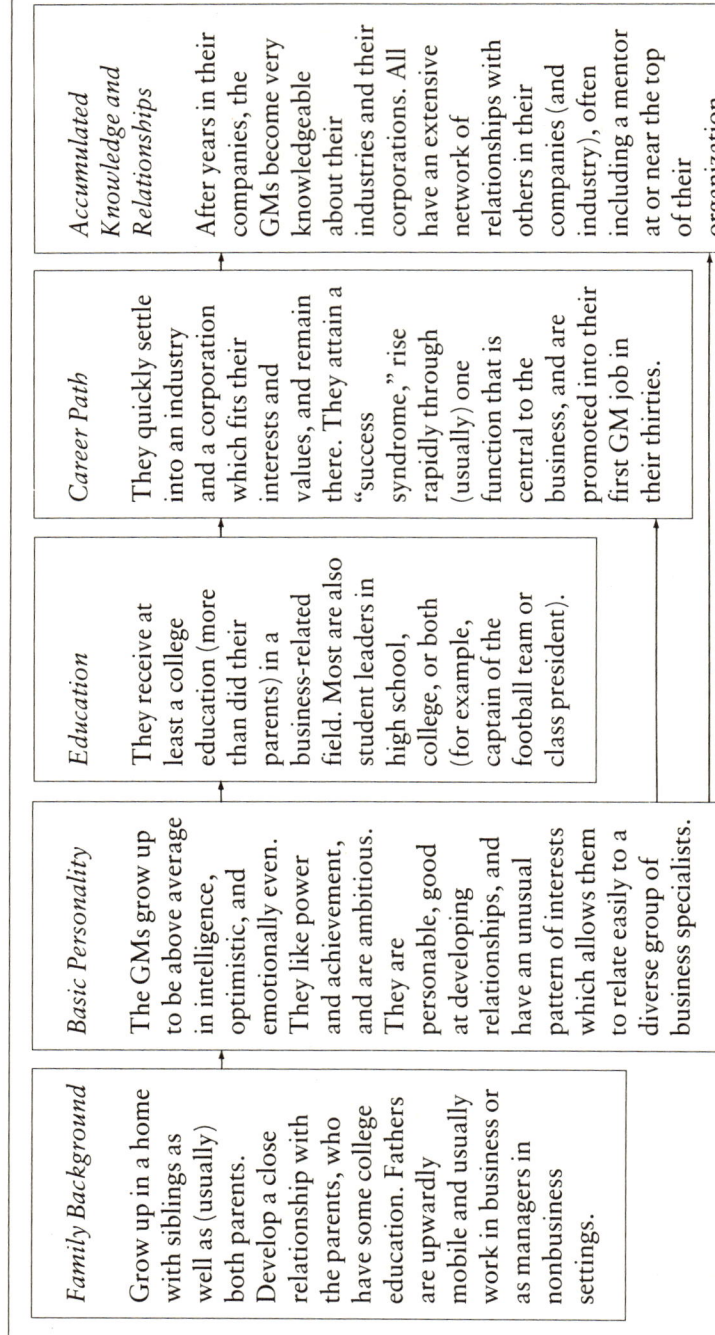

Figure 1-1. *The Development of Effective General Managers*

Source: From J. P. Kotter, *The General Managers* (New York: Free Press, 1982). Reprinted with permission.

taught on the firing line, by demanding assignments, by good or bad bosses, and by mistakes and setbacks and misfortune. Maybe executives are blessed with characteristics that give them the edge in learning these things, but *learn* them they must.

Leaders: Growing Talent

Kotter concluded that it takes ten to twenty years to "grow" a general manager.[11] It is the thesis of this book that development during that time depends not just on raw talent but also on the experiences one has and what one does with them. Specifically, not all experiences are created equal. Some experiences simply pack more developmental wallop than others. Further, the lessons that these experiences might teach are not random. Certain things are more likely to be learned from one kind of experience than from another.

We will suggest that corporations' use of experience to develop executive talent has been a seat-of-the-pants operation. Companies viewed as better managed seem to do more of it than less well-managed companies,[12] but our knowledge of how experience develops managers has been primitive at best. This book will describe some of the experiences that senior executives believe changed them as managers and the lessons they took from them. It will suggest ways that the developmental potential of a work experience might be assessed, examine the different learning demands that experience can make, suggest some ways in which managers might make more of the experiences they have, and finally give suggestions for organizations to make better use of experience as a developmental tool.

How Do We Know?

Science does not often lend itself to absolutes. Even in physics, just when we thought we had a truth, Newtonian mechanics came up short.[13] In some ways the social sciences are even more ambiguous, still groping for the right questions, much less definitive answers. In one lively meeting with human resource professionals from corporations that sponsor our research, we faced a fair question: "We don't have enough executive bench strength for the future; how can we grow enough talent to lead this company in the years ahead?"

That question, posed to us in 1981, started us down a tortuous research path that went from interviews to open-ended surveys to mailed questionnaires, that started with three but eventually involved more than a dozen Fortune 500 corporations, that repeatedly found us on the firing line working with human resource professionals and senior line executives to actually implement the findings. This book is an amalgam of those experiences, but its core lies in data from four separate studies,[14] encompassing 191 successful executives[15] from six major corporations[16] who responded to some version of the following question:

> When you think about your career as a manager, certain events or episodes probably stand out in your mind—things that led to a lasting change in you as a manager. Please identify at least three key events in your career, things that made a difference in the way you manage now.
>
> 1. What happened?
> 2. What did you learn from it (for better or worse)?

The answers we received yielded descriptions of 616 events and 1,547 corresponding lessons.[17] The experiences could be broadly described as assignments (specific jobs they were given to do), bosses (other people who had impact in their own right), and hardships (setbacks and tough times), which constitute chapters 2, 3, and 4 of this book.

The Lessons of Experience

Throughout this book we will refer to "lessons" executives said they learned from their experiences. These lessons as a whole seem to represent some fundamental executive skills and ways of thinking that can be discussed thematically. Figure 1–2 lists

Setting and Implementing Agendas
- Technical/professional skills
- All about the business one is in
- Strategic thinking
- Shouldering full responsibility
- Building and using structure and control systems
- Innovative problem-solving methods

Handling Relationships
- Handling political situations
- Getting people to implement solutions
- What executives are like
- How to work with executives
- Strategies of negotiation
- Dealing with people over whom you have no authority
- Understanding other people's perspectives
- Dealing with conflict
- Directing and motivating subordinates
- Developing other people
- Confronting subordinate performance problems
- Managing former bosses and peers

Basic Values
- You can't manage everything all alone
- Sensitivity to the human side of management
- Basic management values

Executive Temperament
- Being tough when necessary
- Self-confidence
- Coping with situations beyond your control
- Persevering through adversity
- Coping with ambiguous situations
- Use (and abuse) of power

Personal Awareness
- The balance between work and personal life
- Knowing what really excites you about work
- Personal limits and blind spots
- Taking charge of your career
- Recognizing and seizing opportunities

See Esther Lindsey, Virginia Homes, and M. W. McCall, Jr., *Key Events in Executives' Lives,* Technical Report No. 32 (Greensboro, N.C.: Center for Creative Leadership, 1987), p. 227.

Figure 1–2. *The Potential Lessons of Experience*

the specific kinds of lessons executives told us about, grouped by these themes.[18]

The first theme, containing six discrete lessons, is similar to what John Kotter called "agenda setting."[19] He used this term deliberately to distinguish between the ways general managers actually determine direction and the formal strategic planning process. General managers' agendas contained "loosely connected goals and plans" addressing a range of time frames, covering a broad range of business issues, and including both "vague and specific goals and plans."[20] They were only loosely related to formal plans. The constellation of lessons that might enable executives to set short- and long-term agendas involves business and technical knowledge, organizational design skills, thinking broadly and accepting responsibility for direction, and finding alternative ways to accomplish one's ends.

The second cluster in figure 1-2 contains the lessons of relationships. Obviously, working with and through other people lies at the very heart of management. While the core ability in this theme is understanding other people's points of view, the variety of lessons represented in this theme suggests that *different* skills may be required for handling relationships with different kinds of people. Dealing successfully with a subordinate who used to be a boss is a qualitatively different relationship to handle than negotiating with a foreign government, for example. In this sense, there does not seem to be a single interpersonal skill. Senior executives must develop a variety of interpersonal skills appropriate to the variety in the types of people and situations they face.

Basic values, a third theme, contains three lessons that might be viewed as guiding principles with pervasive behavioral implications. While people obviously enter organizations with established values, these values and the new ones formed by experience in the organization are constantly tested and shaped by the situations that play out in the organizational environment.

The fourth constellation of lessons, executive temperament, reflects what an executive is "made of." It captures some of the personal qualities necessary to cope with the demands and ambiguities of executive jobs. This includes the abilities needed to tell the difference between a situation one can't control and one that can be influenced by personal action, to determine when to be tough and when to show compassion, when to be flexible and when to hold the line.

Finally, five lessons seem to reflect a theme we might call personal insight. All the lessons involve self-awareness, whether balancing work and personal life, knowing what one wants out of work, or recognizing one's blind spots and weaknesses.

It's one thing to make a list of lessons, quite another to master them. These lessons are not delivered with spellbinding clarity; they must be dug out of complex, confusing, ambiguous situations. Even when they are delivered up, they are tough to incorporate. Especially for executives, learning is a murky business, occurring in fits and starts over time. Lessons accumulate, evolve, affect one another, gain potency in combination, don't take the first time, atrophy, and get forgotten. Some are much tougher to learn that others, and the toughest part of all may be using what one has learned to make a difference on the job.

Fortunately, these lessons and the themes that hold them together are not just a menu of innate qualities that everyone wishes he had. The lessons are associated with particular experiences, and draw their meaning from that context. For example, learning to direct and motivate subordinates is something executives learned about from several sources (see chapter 2), including starting an operation from scratch and rescuing a business in trouble. In a start-up, the lessons of directing and motivating had to do with inspiring others by working side by side with them, providing strong direction in the face of ambiguity, and persevering in the face of obstacles. The manager had to learn how to motivate an inexperienced team in a situation where no one really knew what he was doing. In contrast, turning an ailing business around involves overcoming resistance and incompetence to get people to do what the manager wants them to do. In these situations, *direct* and *motivate* mean persuading, manipulating, or coercing people. If start-ups teach motivating, then turn-arounds teach directing. So, the listlike quality of the lessons can mask a deeper and richer meaning, a meaning textured by context and amplified by the interwoven nature of learning.

In this book we attempt to preserve this richer meaning by presenting the lessons in the context of the events that spawned them. Listed in figure 1–3, these developmental experiences resulted from our content analysis of the 616 events described to us. Subsequent chapters will deal with them in detail.

As events are discussed, we list the specific lessons associated with them, and we describe the lessons in terms of their domi-

---

Setting the Stage
- Early work experience
- First supervisory job

Leading by Persuasion
- Project/task force assignments
- Line to staff switches

Leading on Line
- Starting from scratch
- Turning a business around
- Managing a larger scope

When Other People Matter
- Bosses

Hardships
- Personal trauma
- Career setback
- Changing jobs
- Business mistakes
- Subordinate performance problems

*Two events, "purely personal" and "values playing out," will not be discussed explicitly in this book. They are, however, described in detail in Esther Lindsey et al., *Key Events in Executives' Lives,* Technical Report No. 32 (Greensboro, N.C.: Center for Creative Leadership, 1987). A final event, "coursework," is addressed in chapter 6.

Figure 1–3. *The Developmental Events**

nant thrust, by which we mean that the individual lessons considered as a whole take on a meaning somewhat different from any single piece. Turn-arounds, for example, were an important source (according to executives) of eleven distinct lessons, including shouldering responsibility, dealing with people over whom one has no authority, and confronting subordinate performance problems. The thrust of these lessons was more than the sum of their parts. Their essential meaning was twofold: on the one hand, learning how to be tough and persuasive; on the other, being tough and instrumental. Figures presented in the discussion of each event will repeat figure 1–2, highlighting the specific lessons that executives said they learned[21] and summarizing our interpretation of the thrust of these lessons taken as a whole.

The Significance of Experience in Executive Development

This chapter began with the assertion that on-the-job development, while widely recognized as important, has not received the kind of research attention that allows us to make the best use of it. Kotter concluded that the firms he studied, all with reputations for having superior managements, were doing a better job of attracting, developing, retaining, and motivating their leadership talent. In describing the varied activities these firms use to develop their talent, he points out first that they focus "scarce development resources on those who have the most potential." How do they meet their developmental needs? By, among other things, "adding responsibilities to jobs, creating special jobs, using inside and outside training, transferring people between functions and divisions, mentoring and coaching employees, giving those people feedback on development progress, and giving them instruction in how to manage their own development."[22]

These kinds of things sound infinitely reasonable until one begins to do them. What kinds of responsibilities should one add to a job to make it developmental? What kind of job should I create—what elements should it have? What kind of training should I send people to, and what should I expect them to get out of it? Should I routinely rotate people between divisions and functions, or only under special circumstances (and if so, what circumstances are those)? Should we set up mentoring programs or training programs to teach our managers to coach? What feedback should we give, and who should give it? What does it mean for people to manage their own development in a for-profit organization?

The executives we studied provided answers to some of these questions, filled in some gaps in our knowledge about learning, suggested why some developmental experiences are more useful than others, and provided some surprising opinions about some of the assumptions we make about development. By looking closely at the assignments that made a difference to these executives, one gets a sense of what constitutes job challenge, and sees that adding to the scope of a job is only one of several developmental options (chapter 2, chapter 5). By looking at what drives development and where people get their knowledge of how the business works, one sees that job rotation for its own sake can be a wasteful process and that cross-boundary movement is justified only when the business plan calls for certain new skills or when specific managerial challenges are available only across a boundary (chapter 6).[23]

As it turns out, training experiences that made the most difference frequently hinged on timing, such that whatever was being learned had a direct bearing on something the executive wanted to accomplish. Somewhat surprisingly, the most potent lessons from the classroom involved increased self-confidence (chapter 5).

Mentoring, in the sense of long-term apprentice/teacher relationships, was rare or nonexistent among these successful senior executives. Between their own rapid advancement and the movement of their bosses, they were seldom with the same person for as long as three years. What seemed to matter was almost the opposite anyway: exposure to a variety of bosses, good and bad, who possessed exceptional qualities of various kinds (chapter 3).

Developmental feedback is a good idea, and delivered constructively by a respected source is no doubt useful. But where executives said they gained insight into themselves and their strengths and weaknesses was not typically from counseling sessions. The lessons of humility were more often generated from their mistakes, confrontations with problem subordinates, traumatic events, and career setbacks (chapter 4).

Helping people take charge of their own development is, appropriately enough, one of the two major purposes of this book. By understanding the rich variety of experience and what it has to offer, aspiring managers and executives can make better decisions regarding career moves and make better use of the lessons their experiences offer to them. But in any organization there are limits to how much control the individual can exert. Like it or not, businesses are not in business primarily to develop people, and development will always be a secondary goal. So the second major purpose of this book is to help organizations do a better job of development by making more efficient and thoughtful use of the developmental experiences they have to offer their high-potential managers.

Perhaps the major advantage of this research and its implications is that they are *not* revolutionary. They take what better managed companies and successful executives are already doing instinctively, and build on it. Somehow we already know that when we are stretched, when we need to learn something new in order to achieve something we care about, we are much more likely to learn it. Left to our own devices, the learners among us will challenge ourselves, and organizations routinely throw talented people into tough situations "to see what they are made of." What this research teaches us is that these practices are in the right direction, but that what makes something developmental and what we learn from developmental experiences are not random. They have some order, some predictability. We can do a better job of identifying, creating, and enriching experiences for purposes of development, and we can predict, at least generally, what kinds of things might be learned from various experiences.

2
Trial by Fire: Learning from Job Assignments[1]

He watched from the helicopter door as laborers clutching chain saws were lowered into the jungle below. For several days the snarl of the saws rose up from the canopy, until at last a landing area large enough to accommodate a helicopter had been cleared. This task constituted the "ground breaking" for the new plant on the Amazon. It was indicative of difficulties to come.

He was responsible for everything—two thousand laborers, costs, results. He had to deal with a hostile left-wing government in a language he had learned only after arriving there. He had to fight disease, contend with political riots, and stand by as his meticulous plans were dashed by capricious officials. Yet, despite these adverse circumstances, the plant got built and is in operation today.

Quite an experience. The stuff of learning by doing. But what, in fact, did this manager learn from his assignment in the jungle? "Oh, part of it was that you really find out if you can manage when you lock up with a foreign government, because they can tell you to go to hell in a second. Other things? I don't know, so many I can't describe them, but overwhelmingly a sense that if I could survive this, nothing would ever hurt that way again."

This was one of over three hundred stories about an assignment that made a difference and what difference it made to a successful corporate executive. Specifically, this is one of thirty-four start-ups, where a manager had to bring something new into existence. In this case, as was true for almost all the assignments described to us, the driving force for learning was job challenge.

While our study is concerned with the relationship between challenge and learning, there is quite a bit of evidence both in our studies and elsewhere[2] that mastering challenging assignments is related to later management success. Bray and his associates[3] at AT&T found that job challenges, stress of assignments, and unstructured assignments were associated with management success, leading them to conclude that stability in the face of stress and uncertainty was a major factor in management progress.

Other studies reached related conclusions. MacKinnon[4] commented on the importance of assigning managers to challenging tasks that tax their capabilities, and Kotter[5] documented that better managed companies in fact do so routinely. Jennings[6] said that crises (certainly one kind of challenge) show what managers can do under stress and can transform potential talent into actual talent. Schein[7] took this a step further by suggesting that one of the most important managerial competencies is the ability to deal emotionally with tough situations such as making decisions under risk and uncertainty, acting in a crisis, being responsible for the acts of others, and occasionally firing people. This argument receives further support from Grey and Gordon,[8] who found that risk-oriented managers were more likely to get to the top, and stay that way once they got there. Hambrick[9] found that executives who could cope with uncertainty had greater power within their organizations.

It's one thing to document the idea that job challenge in its various forms is important, but it's quite another to find evidence of where the skills to handle challenge are learned or what learning results from different challenges. Relevant lessons are referred to (comments on the importance of dealing laterally and upwards, for example), but we could find only a few studies that tried to explain how successful managers learned them.[10] Studies of failure do point to lessons not learned. Skinner and Sasser[11] found that ineffective managers tolerated ineffective subordinates and lacked boldness and nerve. A survey of corporate executives by Allen[12] identified indecisiveness, lack of initiative, and failure to take responsibility as important shortcomings.

In summary, many researchers agree that job challenge and specifically difficult assignments are indeed the best teacher of up-and-coming executives. Kotter[13] found that the companies with the best reputations for good management made extensive use of job challenge to develop their talent. In this chapter we will describe in detail the kinds of assignments that challenged executives in our study, and the kinds of things they say they learned as a result.

The executives we studied were well into their careers, aged from early to middle forties, on average. In recalling the experiences that had made lasting changes in them, most were spanning a period of more than twenty years. Because we asked them to describe only three events from this long career, we are confident that the ones they chose were indeed potent.

Some executives vividly recalled experiences from the very beginnings of their careers—an *early work* experience in some technical or functional specialty or their *first supervisory job*. These experiences sometimes set the stage for later, more dramatic challenges.

Many executives described assignments where the primary challenge was to lead by persuading others. These included *project and task force* jobs that were discrete, temporary assignments on major problems facing an organization. Aimed at a specific outcome over a few months to a year, these jobs were typically taken on as short-term assignments in addition to one's current job. Persuasion-centered assignments also included *line-to-staff switches,* in which managers left line jobs, in which they had been in charge and their results had been measurable, for a stint in a staff role. Whether in corporate offices or a division, developmental staff assignments required managers to learn a new technical area—market research, strategic planning, or financial planning, for example. Most managers found such assignments intellectually challenging and a little scary.

Then there were assignments, like the one that started this chapter, where the premium was placed on individual, full-responsibility leadership. *Starting from scratch,* managers created a business venture from nothing or almost nothing. They found themselves accountable for the success of building new plants, introducing product lines, starting new businesses, opening new markets, or creating subsidiaries. Others described *fix-it/turn-it-around jobs.* In these assignments, managers were sent to dismantle and reconstruct existing operations plagued with maladies. They took over utter messes with unskilled staff, unwanted products, or chaotic operations. Typically, they were under a mandate to reorganize the operation, but equally typically, no one was quite sure how this could be accomplished. And then there was the most commonly reported experience, *a leap in scope.* This involved an increase in responsibility that was both broader than and different from what had gone before. Leaps in scope, at their extreme, involved moves into totally new businesses and, at the same time, massive increases in numbers of people, dollars, and functions to manage.

As we will see in this chapter, it's not the assignments per se that drive development. Each of these assignments represents a particular constellation of elements that defines it. It's what the manager has to do in, for example, a fix-it that causes the stretch: coming up with strategies that will save the business while overcoming inadequacies of the staff. We call these central challenges and demands the "core elements" of an experience, and it is they that, in our opinion, drive learning. The difference between a developmental task force and one that is quickly forgotten may lie in the presence or absence of certain core elements. So as we discuss each type of assignment (and later other experiences as well), we'll talk about the elements that comprise it and, we believe, that provide the learning opportunity. In chapter 5 we will pull all these elements together and suggest that any job can be developmental to the degree that some of these elements are present. In short, there's no magic in fix-its or scopes or any of the assignments. They are the place where special blends of challenges force a manager to learn or fail.

Setting the Stage

The importance of *early* job challenge, as was noted in the previous section, has been well documented in numerous research studies and journal articles. One review of the research on this topic, for example, concluded: "Considerable evidence suggests that initial experience in the organization, such as the first regular assignments, can have an important effect on later career outcomes."[14]

In a survey of more than seven hundred chief executives, conducted by Charles Margerison and Andrew Kakabadse for the American Management Association, "early leadership experience" received a high ranking among the key influences on their career development. According to these CEOs, leadership is a practical skill that can be learned only through actual experience, preferably before the age of thirty.[15]

The reason for this, as many researchers have found, is that little of what is taught in college or even business schools really prepares would-be managers for the realities of managing. As William F. Dowling concluded, "There's no book they can consult to find out what to do."[16] In another study, 73 percent of the graduates surveyed reported that their MBA skills were used "only marginally or not at all" in their first managerial assignments. The study concluded that "one learns to be a leader by serving as a leader."[17]

Many studies of managerial performance have found that the most critical skill for beginning managers, and one most often lacking, is interpersonal competence, or the ability to deal with "people problems." Few college or business school graduates have learned how to motivate subordinates, how to persuade or influence colleagues, or how to overcome resistance to their ideas by "selling upward" in an organization.

In his book *Career Dynamics,* Edgar H. Schein pointed out that most new managers feel much more comfortable with technical problems than with people problems.[18] In fact, many seem to feel that people problems are an "illegitimate" use of their time and unworthy of their efforts. This attitude, Schein noted, must be "unlearned" if they hope to have a career in management.

For those who do succeed in their first managerial jobs, however, success can be addictive, and thus doubly rewarding, as Douglas Bray and Ann Howard found in their long-term "Management Progress Study" at AT&T. "As they achieved," Howard said of a group of Bell System managers, "they experienced pleasure—a feeling that motivated them to want to achieve more. Their competence and self-confidence increased, which in turn encouraged them to tackle more difficult problems."[19]

The lasting impact of early job challenge was apparent in our sample of executives. Even though early work experiences and first supervisory jobs were long ago and far away, many executives still considered them to have been pivotal developmental experiences. Those who recounted them seemed to have gotten from them a head start in the basics—lessons in how things work in an organization as opposed to what they had learned in the classroom, and lessons in dealing with people. These kinds of lessons reappeared in other experiences, usually in more sophisticated forms or under more difficult conditions, but for some executives the early exposure was extremely useful later on—so useful, in fact, that some executives expressed regret that new hires no longer go through some of the same initiations.

Early Work Experiences

> When I was a young man, and first came to work for [the company], I began as a field engineer in South Texas. They gave me a $25 raise, a flashlight, and just said, "Go to work."
>
> My job out there was to keep an oil and gas field flowing twenty-four hours a day. Frankly, it was a lot cheaper for them to take a young man like me, whom you paid by the month, and put him out there in the fields, than to keep a bunch of maintenance people doing regular repairs on the equipment.
>
> So when the cold winters came, and the lines would freeze up, I would get calls all through the night. The most significant thing I remember about that job was I just never slept a lot. We weren't paid a lot, and we worked real hard. But you know, I was young, and you can do those kinds of things when you're young. But I think those five years keeping that field going did a lot for me personally. I learned to work with a lot of different people, and the importance of developing loyalties with them. It also taught me a real work discipline, and it made some people in the company say, "You know, he's not afraid of hard work."
>
> You know, when I got out of school, I was just like every other youngster there. I didn't know the basis for the oil field or

how the pumps and engines worked. But putting in the kind of hours I did, and being out there by myself at three o'clock in the morning trying to make something work when you really want to go home and go to bed, I really learned a lot. I was making decisions. Not big decisions; just little decisions about repairing things. But I had to make the decisions myself, about how to repair it and how to get it going without blowing things up. Just working alone out there in the field, in the cold winter nights, I learned a lot.

I think that's one of the problems we have today with young people: we don't let them go through that kind of tough learning experience. We take them right out of school, and right away put them behind desks as engineers. We immediately start giving them projects to work on. But frankly, they don't have the background or the opportunities they should of working out in the field, repairing those pumps and engines themselves, and making things work when they don't even know how they work. That's really a valuable experience that they're missing.

Early work experiences described as developmental were debuts in the world of business or organizations. Whether they took place in engineering, accounting, the military, or the oil field, these experiences were characterized by three basic elements: a "first exposure" to the realities of an organization (it was cheaper to keep the oil field running with someone you paid by the month); some kind of confrontation with these realities, especially those aspects outside one's technical specialty ("I didn't know the basis for the oil field or how the pumps and engines worked"); and the discovery that working with other people—customers, colleagues, or bosses ("I learned to work with a lot of different people, and the importance of developing loyalties with them")—could be problematic.

The lessons these people learned from their first jobs and early work experiences—such as how to manage one's own time or how to get along with other people—might seem obvious to those who have spent many years in management. But to young people just starting out, these were valuable lessons, ones they carried with them throughout their later careers. They included an assortment of observations about the reality of organizations that might best be called "welcome to the world of work," some realizations about people, and some realizations about themselves.

Welcome to the World of Work. For many of the people we interviewed, these jobs were their first ones after completing school, and the sharp transition from student to employee often brought a rough awakening to the reality of work. It might be learning to go without sleep in the oil field, or learning "that the business world isn't always 'fair,' and that good luck and knowing the right people can be just as important at times as hard work."

"After leaving the university," another executive recalled, "I worked for three years with an accounting firm. I had to move from the pure academic life, which I really enjoyed, to an environment of high pressure, long hours, and some abuse from senior people. It was like being educated all over again—at times a very frustrating experience."

All in all, the thrust of these lessons was simple: People discovered that they hadn't learned in school all they needed to know. Organizations were a new world.

People 101: An Introduction to People at Work. Many of these young people had done quite well in college but were surprised to discover that their new jobs required much more than intellectual skills: "The only goal I'd had in school," one told us, "was to do well and get good grades at whatever I was doing. But work was a rude shock. In college, if I made an 86 on an exam, it meant I knew most of the right answers. But at work, I found out that knowing the right answer was only 10 percent of the battle: working with people was the other 90 percent. And we hadn't learned that at school."

Even in these mostly nonmanagerial jobs, often before they even dreamed of rising to managerial ranks themselves, these people—at least those who kept their eyes open—learned some valuable lessons about dealing with other people. As one put it, "I learned how people in the factory feel about their jobs, and what makes them want to do a better job, and what makes them not care." Another told us, "I learned that people are basically the same, from the janitor on the shop floor to the secretaries to the plant manager. They all want to be treated the same: with respect, and with recognition for their achievements."

Gaining an understanding for the feelings of others was a frequent theme in the recollections of the executives in our study, and many claimed that they later put that knowledge to good use in their own careers as managers. As one told us, "I gained an appreciation of the hourly worker's point of view. I learned what is important to him, why he thinks as he does, and why it's important to be honest and straightforward with him. This knowledge helped me tremendously later, when I became a manager myself."

Insight into Self. Successfully meeting their first challenges at work gave some of these future executives a shot of self-confidence. Even if they weren't five years of keeping an oil field running without blowing it up, early jobs could result in a strong sense of self that helped them approach much tougher assignments later in their careers with a can-do spirit. As one explained, "Handling a wide variety of tasks, and doing them well, gave me a feeling of self-confidence and earned the respect of the senior manager." Another told us, "I learned that through my own energy and intelligence I could compete successfully with more experienced colleagues. That gave me a great deal of confidence in myself and my ability."

One advantage of developmental early work experiences was that they sometimes offered a chance to learn about different parts of the business—without the pressure and responsibility of management. As one fellow explained, looking back on such a relatively carefree time, "I was able to take risks and try new approaches without serious penalties if I made a mistake."

For many who described early work experiences, the confidence came from seeing that they had the ability to adapt. Some saw that they could figure out how to accomplish assigned tasks when they lacked the specific skills or knowledge supposedly necessary to do the job. In other words, they learned to learn while doing, or to make do by using or adapting the skills and knowledge they did have in new contexts. As one person put it, "I found that I could roll with the punches, learn from mistakes, deal with uncertainty. I learned to focus on what's really important, to sense which of thirty brush fires might become a real forest fire, and to deal with that one first."

Sometimes these early experiences provided the confidence of learning what one did or did not want out of a career. "After one year of disenchantment with college," one executive told us, "I started working in a factory on the production line. But after six months there I returned to school during the day, while working full-time on the night shift. I decided I wanted to become part of the factory management because I felt there had to be better ways to manage people."

Another executive, a former engineer, recalled: "Changing jobs at that time taught me that I was much more suited to production than quality control, which is what I had trained for. I also learned that production had much more impact on the business. And I realized that if I wanted to get anywhere in that business, that's where I should be. That job set the direction for the rest of my career."

Not all of these early work experiences were glamorous, but even the dismal could teach valuable lessons. In some cases, the very boredom of the early jobs helped these young people discover that they wanted more from their careers than "just a job," or just making a living. "After college," one said, "I worked for a small accounting firm in my home town. But the constant daily routine and the lack of depth of the partners of the firm had a great impact in arousing me to think about my future and what I wanted to do with my life. I decided to go back to school and get an advanced degree so that I wouldn't be stuck in low-level jobs."

So, as summarized in figure 2-1, early nonmanagerial experiences offered a smorgasbord of learning that, for some, set the stage for later "big time" challenges. In a similar way, many executives were introduced to organizational realities by their first managerial job.

Individual Lessons

Setting and Implementing Agendas
- Technical/professional skills
- All about the business one is in
- **STRATEGIC THINKING**
- Shouldering full responsibility
- Building and using structure and control systems
- **INNOVATIVE PROBLEM-SOLVING METHODS**

Handling Relationships
- Handling political situations
- **GETTING PEOPLE TO IMPLEMENT SOLUTIONS**
- What executives are like
- How to work with executives
- **STRATEGIES OF NEGOTIATION**
- Dealing with people over whom you have no authority
- Understanding other people's perspectives
- Dealing with conflict
- Directing and motivating subordinates
- Developing other people
- Confronting subordinate performance problems
- Managing former bosses and peers

Basic Values
- You can't manage everything all alone
- Sensitivity to the human side of management
- Basic management values

Executive Temperament
- **BEING TOUGH WHEN NECESSARY**
- Self-confidence
- Coping with situations beyond your control
- Persevering through adversity
- **COPING WITH AMBIGUOUS SITUATIONS**
- Use (and abuse) of power

(Continued)

Figure 2–1. *The Potential Lessons of Early Work Experience*

Personal Awareness
- The balance between work and personal life
- Knowing what really excites you about work
- Personal limits and blind spots
- Taking charge of your career
- Recognizing and seizing opportunities

Major Learning Thrusts
- Transition to the world of work. A series of doses of reality—awareness that there is much to learn that wasn't taught in school.
- People at work. Insights into how people are different and what motivates them.
- Insight into self. Confidence in their ability to do things in an organization and to handle new situations.

See Esther Lindsey, Virginia Homes, and M.W. McCall, Jr., *Key Events in Executives' Lives,* Technical Report No. 32 (Greensboro, N.C.: Center for Creative Leadership, 1987), 191, 202.

Figure 2-1. (*Continued*)

The First Supervisory Job

At age 24, I was promoted to my first managerial position as office services manager, with no advance notice—not even a hint it was to happen. I replaced an individual who had had a heart attack, and who had held the position for 15 years. I had absolutely no experience in managing anything at that time, and I was suddenly responsible for supplying a 600-person operation.

I quickly found out that knowing the technically right answer was much easier than selling it to and working with the people who had to implement it. To succeed as a manager, I had to abandon the nitty-gritty details of engineering. I gradually realized that you can be competent without trying to know more than your people about what they do.

I also learned that when managing your peers and friends, you have to consider their feelings. You have to realize you can't make everybody happy, and you can't always win. At least some of them will believe they should really be in your position. But most people do want leadership, and they will respond to someone who knows where he's going. I learned an important lesson then: that leadership contributes just as much as engineering to the success of an organization.

For some people in our study, one of their most developmental experiences was their managerial debut as a low-level supervisor or department head, either in a corporation or in a branch of the military. For these people, it was in their first supervisory job that they discovered that there's more to this managing business than technical knowledge or corporate procedure manuals. Some of them also learned that responsibility for even a small group or department means figuring out how its activities—and their own decisions—are necessarily linked to those of the larger organization. Seeing the world from this broader perspective gave some their first taste of thinking strategically.

But while there were lessons in seeing how the parts fit and concocting plans and strategies, the primary thrust of learning from first supervisory jobs was about people.

As future executives move from the ranks of individual contributors to a first supervisory position, the most obvious lesson to be learned is that management itself is a distinct and complex skill quite different from competence in a technical area. For some, this skill of getting people to do what you want seems to come naturally. For others, it was something they learned, often slowly and sometimes painfully.

In order to manage effectively, these new supervisors first had to learn to become aware of and sensitive to the psychological needs of the people they supervised. Those whose previous training and experience had been limited to the narrow confines of sales, technology, or finance were often surprised to discover that their employees could not be treated like numbers in a chemical equation. Getting people to do what needed to be done was a psychologically difficult task, one that required them to learn many new skills, such as gaining the respect and confidence of one's subordinates, one of the essential requirements of leadership. Engineers (of whom there were many in our sample) seemed to have a particularly difficult time making the switch from solving technical problems to solving human problems, perhaps because people simply aren't subject to the rigorous laws of logic or measurable with the precision that engineers are accustomed to. One engineer just promoted to his first management position learned the hard way:

> When I first became a supervisor of a group of development engineers, I looked at management like an engineer would. I read all about performance reviews, and boy was I ready to give performance reviews. I told them in detail all the things they did wrong, and all the things they did right. No one had ever given them that kind of feedback before. But I just about killed those engineers, and nearly crushed the morale of that organization. I was clearly not a skilled coacher of people. So I went out and got some help. I finally learned that just as you had to know the laws of physics to be a good engineer, I had to know the laws of psychology to be a good manager.
>
> This was a tremendous lesson for me: that you can't just translate the skills of one profession to another. When you're going into a new profession, you'd better learn as much as you can about it before you jump. Take as much time as you can learning the differences so that you don't use your own experience when it really doesn't apply.

First-time supervisors learned that problems in dealing with people came in many forms. For example, the experience of supervising older subordinates was a common one for many young officers in the military service, and their superior rank alone did not solve the problem.

> My first supervisory experience came as a new lieutenant just out of ROTC, at age twenty-one. I was made section leader for eighteen people, nearly all my senior in age and experience. At first I tried to lead, but it was a catastrophe. It took me about a year to learn that a leader is there to serve the people who work for him, and I lost some friends in this learning process. This experience did more than anything since to shape my attitude toward leadership.

For those who had never had such responsibility, the problems of people management often seemed deceptively simple. But the basic lesson of first supervision was that people can present problems. "I learned that people are different," one told us, "and that you can't manage everyone the same way."

In their previous nonmanagerial jobs, some of these young people had already discovered that simply getting along with people at work had been an important learning experience. Now, however, as managers, they had to learn how to lead them, a skill at which few had ever received any training. The potential lessons of their first supervisory experiences are summarized in figure 2-2.

Curtain Call

Whether the early job was managerial or not, the developmental legacy was fundamental. Organizations are a different animal, and working in them is another education. People come in all shapes and sizes—and working effectively with them starts with understanding them. Basic lessons, taught in what will later seem a relatively simple setting. Basic lessons that will reappear in more demanding situations, that will get more complicated and sophisticated, that appear deceptively simple at first.

The reason the lessons will get tougher is that the situations get tougher too. Early work experiences may seem demanding, and at the time they certainly can be, but their core elements are simple compared to later challenges an executive may face. But for those lucky enough to have had developmentally valuable early experiences, their grounding in the basics served them well as the stakes grew larger.

Leading by Persuasion

Even when early work experiences were later seen as important developmental events, their demands were either nonmanagerial or the most basic of managerial/supervisory challenges. Typically, the more complicated managerial lessons didn't come until

Individual Lessons

Setting and Implementing Agendas
- Technical/professional skills
- All about the business one is in
- **STRATEGIC THINKING**
- **SHOULDERING FULL RESPONSIBILITY**
- Building and using structure and control systems
- Innovative problem-solving methods

Handling Relationships
- Handling political situations
- **GETTING PEOPLE TO IMPLEMENT SOLUTIONS**
- What executives are like
- How to work with executives
- Strategies of negotiation
- Dealing with people over whom you have no authority
- Understanding other people's perspectives
- Dealing with conflict
- Directing and motivating subordinates
- Developing other people
- Confronting subordinate performance problems
- **MANAGING FORMER BOSSES AND PEERS**

Basic Values
- You can't manage everything all alone
- **SENSITIVITY TO THE HUMAN SIDE OF MANAGEMENT**
- Basic management values

Executive Temperament
- Being tough when necessary
- Self-confidence
- Coping with situations beyond your control
- Persevering through adversity
- Coping with ambiguous situations
- Use (and abuse) of power

Personal Awareness
- The balance between work and personal life
- Knowing what really excites you about work

> - Personal limits and blind spots
> - Taking charge of your career
> - Recognizing and seizing opportunities
>
> *Major Learning Thrusts*
>
> Management is different from technical work: Learning to deal effectively with people is at the heart of management.
>
> See Esther Lindsey, et al., *Key Events in Executives' Lives,* Technical Report No. 32 (Greensboro, N.C.: Center for Creative Leadership, 1987), 203–213.

Figure 2–2. *The Potential Lessons of First Supervisory Experience*

the situations grew more demanding and complex. Ironically, some of the toughest leadership situations required getting other people to do things when they didn't have to, and maybe didn't want to. But unlike the milder versions encountered in early jobs, the demands for these skills and the stakes escalated dramatically in some projects and task forces and many staff jobs, where responsibility and authority seldom align and where figuring out who's in charge can be a hopeless undertaking.

Throughout their careers, effective executives have to be able to persuade and influence other people, in addition to exercising their legitimate authority. These two kinds of experience—projects/task forces and line-to-staff switches—can provide the opportunity to learn these skills. But they also have the added benefit of forcing managers to view the world from a different perspective. Looking at a product or project in great depth, as might happen in a staff analyst role, can stand in stark contrast to the "proficient superficiality" of the peripatetic line perspective.[20]

It could be argued, in fact, that some of the greatest leadership challenges of all can be found in these nonline assignments. Imagine being given the challenge of making a major recommendation to senior management on an issue of critical strategic importance to the business, based on areas of specialty and expertise about which you know very little, with no direct reports (or just a few staff) on whom to rely, within a ridiculously short period of time, and knowing that your career may depend on the quality of your reasoning (which you have some control over) and the outcome of your recommendation if it's accepted (which you may have no control over).

Developmental Project and Task Force Assignments

Project and task force assignments sometimes got a less-than-enthusiastic reception from managers who later on described them as developmental. The new assignment frequently came on top of, not in place of, an already demanding job, was organizationally significant (and therefore highly visible to upper management), and usually had a finite (and tight) time frame (six months to a year).

Executives told us about three general types of project/task force assignments: trying out new ideas or installing new systems of some kind; negotiating agreements with external parties, such as joint venture partners, unions, or governments; and troubleshooting a problem-filled situation such as a major accident or plant closing. Regardless of the type, each project/task force assignment may as well have been labeled "This is a test." Could managers learn a new skill on the run? Could they cope with groups of people they'd never worked with before? Could they do it quickly? Could they handle the pressure of visible success or failure? Also regardless of type, the lessons from project/task force assignments had two broad thrusts: learning how to handle ignorance (which may be a first for a technical or functional expert), and learning how to get others to cooperate without having authority over them (which can get exceedingly difficult as the stakes get higher).

You Can't Be the Expert on Everything. Many managers begin their careers in a technical or functional specialty such as engineering, law, or finance and rise because of their technical excellence. Project assignments propel them into a world in which their old skills may not mean much, or where others know even more than they do.

One executive, for example, was put on a secret acquisition team to buy out a supplier of computer parts. He knew little about acquisitions, and because of the secret nature of the project he could not openly ask for desperately needed information. Yet, when he began to suspect something wasn't right with the deal, he broke off negotiations—against the advice of his senior management. Later, the company they almost acquired went abruptly out of business, and his judgment was vindicated. He had taken the risk of opposing senior management in an area where he was a novice, and learned from it valuable lessons not only about his ability to handle new situations but also about how important it could be to stand up for himself and his analysis of a situation.

Project assignments like this one place managers at a fork in the road. The easy path is to rely on habit and wear themselves out trying to become an instant technical expert. After all, technical expertise has guaranteed their success so far, and it is easy to see it as the right choice this time. The other path is a dark one that requires diving into the unknown. This path demands that managers give up an illusion of mastery and instead use the skills of others to complete the project.

One executive who took the dark path described his experience this way:

> I was a marketing guy sent to start up the first computerization project our company had ever attempted. In those days, adding machines were our most sophisticated tool. I walked in, not really even knowing what a computer was and faced this group of computer fanatics ready to revolutionize our operations. Maybe my ignorance saved me because how could I posture when I knew nothing? Anyway, this is what I said: "Let me tell you guys three things. One, you've got a leader who knows nothing about computers and a lot about marketing, so we've both got a lot to learn from each other. Two, I'm not afraid to say "I don't know" and ask stupid questions, and don't you be either. Third, let's not

worry about our differences too much. Let's see what we can do to set up this system and while we're at it let's move the art of marketing twenty years into the future.

As sensible as this may seem, managers usually choose the other path. It's more comforting to stay with what we know, or immerse ourselves in the technical details of a new field, while falling back on the ultimate defense of the mediocre manager: "Take no action until all the information is in."

This approach assumes that it's a manager's responsibility to be the expert, to master the content of the assignment, and to direct others accordingly—a technical manager for all seasons, a walking encyclopedia of business brilliance. Some might call this arrogance, and it may be, partly, but more often such a belief results from the fear of giving up control, of being exposed as a nincompoop, or the worse fear of all—being wrong with everyone watching.

Yet the test of a project assignment is not to see if a manager can master a new field in six months. The true test is a crucial one in any complex organization: "Can you *manage* something new without having to *master* it first?" The real test—the one that faced the marketing person with the computer project—is, can you be a quick study and learn to ask the right questions, grasp the basics, and work with others to get the job done?

You've Got to Understand the Other Person's Point of View. The second major learning thrust of project assignments grew out of the need to work with and through others. Lacking the expertise that others had, yet charged with the responsibility for accomplishing the project goals, managers had to find some common ground.

For the marketing manager charged with the computerization project, the goal was to create this common ground by working from two directions. He had to get excited about computers and what they could do for the corporation, and he had to inspire the computer buffs to think of every possible computer application, not just the general administrative and accounting applications they were charged with. By putting together two separate areas of expertise—marketing and computers—they came up with one of the first computer-driven market research packages. "The key all along was to make it clear that we were in this together. I rarely pulled rank even when I disagreed with them. After all, if they didn't know more about what they were doing than I did, we were all in deep trouble."

One way or another, the managers we studied learned that to get things done they had to be able to work with others over whom they had little authority and little control. Furthermore, they learned that having authority and control was not the issue; persuading others through patience and understanding was. Concern for the views of others and melding those into a common goal are what paid off.

Part of the payoff was also increased self-confidence as the managers took stands and handled unfamiliar problems. But the dominant effect of project experiences was a sense of transition. Successfully completing projects bumped the managers from a narrow ("I must be the expert") perspective to the broader one required of a manager. Many admitted to themselves for the first time that they could no longer know every detail nor control every action within a work group. Sometimes leadership boiled down to stopping, asking questions, and listening to other points of view. "You've got to understand *their* point of view—it isn't like yours"; "If you want to get them on your side, you've got to get into their knickers"; "They [Japanese businessmen] won't respect you unless you learn to eat peas with chopsticks." Lessons don't get more concrete than that. (Figure 2–3 summarizes the lessons of project and task force assignments.)

Line-to-Staff Switch

Some of the managers we studied were plucked, even pushed, into one- or two-year assignments in corporate staff roles. All had been in operational jobs where they were responsible for some bottom line numbers. With the switch to a staff assignment, they were suddenly on alien turf. The managers usually relocated to corporate headquarters and reported to or worked with executives several levels up from them, while struggling

Individual Lessons

Setting and Implementing Agendas
- Technical/professional skills
- All about the business one is in
- Strategic thinking
- Shouldering full responsibility
- Building and using structure and control systems
- Innovative problem-solving methods

Handling Relationships
- Handling political situations
- Getting people to implement solutions
- What executives are like
- **HOW TO WORK WITH EXECUTIVES**
- **STRATEGIES OF NEGOTIATION**
- Dealing with people over whom you have no authority
- Understanding other people's perspectives
- **DEALING WITH CONFLICT**
- Directing and motivating subordinates
- Developing other people
- Confronting subordinate performance problems
- Managing former bosses and peers

Basic Values
- You can't manage everything all alone
- Sensitivity to the human side of management
- Basic management values

Executive Temperament
- Being tough when necessary
- **SELF-CONFIDENCE**
- Coping with situations beyond your control
- Persevering through adversity
- **COPING WITH AMBIGUOUS SITUATIONS**
- Use (and abuse) of power

Personal Awareness
- The balance between work and personal life
- Knowing what really excites you about work
- Personal limits and blind spots

Trial by Fire

> - Taking charge of your career
> - Recognizing and seizing opportunities
>
> *Major Learning Thrusts*
>
> *Understanding Other People's Points of View*
>
> Because they lacked others' expertise and often had no control over situations, managers learned to sell, persuade, and ask questions to learn how others thought. They used this knowledge to introduce common goals and strategies to get the project completed.
>
> *Giving Up Technical Mastery*
>
> Managers did quick studies in unfamiliar areas to understand what was important. Their perspective changed from that of an expert doer to that of a manager who gets things done through others.
>
> See Esther Lindsey, et al., *Key Events in Executives' Lives,* Technical Report No. 32 (Greensboro, N.C.: Center for Creative Leadership, 1987), 41–54.

Figure 2–3. *The Potential Lessons of Project and Task Force Assignments*

with a new technical area. The assigned areas were diverse—managers most commonly did stints in planning and financial analysis. Less often they were assigned to general administration, R&D management, training and human resources, and productivity improvement.

The stated purpose of these staff assignments was multiple: to teach managers other sides of the business, to give them an understanding of corporate strategies and culture, and to expose them to the executives who ran the company. But staff assignments made other demands as well. For managers accustomed to finite jobs with finite accountabilities, staff assignments produced anxiety. This was partly because the assignments were conceptual rather than tangible, and strategic rather than tactical. But above all, staff assignments were frustrating, because managerial performance couldn't be measured by the method the managers had come to know and respect—the bottom line. As with project assignments, lessons from switching to a staff role had two major thrusts: learning to cope with ambiguity and understanding corporate strategy and culture.

Learning to Cope with Ambiguity. "I had never been in a position with no bottom line before," one executive recalled. "Although it was intellectually demanding, I had trouble with its sterility—all those numbers were dehumanizing. I did not enjoy the job, although working with the top brass was exciting."

Many managers don't enjoy their time at corporate headquarters, perhaps because they feel that they are not accomplishing anything tangible. They persuade, recommend, and occasionally see things done at their behest. But they are not performing a concrete job. What is perhaps worse, there are no sales figures, production charts, or profit statements to assure them that they are in fact doing a good job.

The managers we studied learned that gathering and synthesizing information was the key in dealing with these ambiguous situations. Like the managers in project assignments, those who switched to staff jobs learned to rely on others, ask questions to find out what was most important, and tackle new technical areas piece by piece. Yet once the information was assimilated, the picture was still incomplete, because they were concocting a scenario of what might be. And that scenario, with all of its uncertainties, usually became the basis of a report or presentation to top management.

Even for the confident, it was unnerving to walk into a room full of executives and expound on topics they had barely known existed six months or a year before. The intellectual challenge coupled with the obvious testing drained them. Many remembered their first presentation to an executive group as a fearful experience.

The presentations counted for something. Whatever the topic, major decisions might be made, and whatever was said had to be crisp, accurate, and insightful. "Information is the executive medium," one executive said. "You'd better be accurate and you'd better believe in what you're saying. It's OK to say 'I don't know,' but it's not OK to back off a point you've carefully prepared. Then people begin to wonder what you're doing there if you have no point of view."

As managers looked back on these presentations, they drew out a lesson: the importance of constructing a point of view and having the courage to present it. The very act of doing this reduced their anxiety and changed their view of ambiguous situations. The ambiguity of not knowing became less something to be feared and more something to be accepted. "Ambiguity just is," said one executive. "You're never going to have all the information, but you have to act anyway."

Learning to Understand Corporate Strategies and Culture. In the course of developmental staff assignments, the managers said they picked up significant technical expertise and began to understand how a business must respond to external conditions—customers, competitors, government regulators, and Wall Street analysts.

Responding and adapting to changes from the outside involved some science and some guesswork. Successful strategy hinged on raising the chances of success a bit by playing out different scenarios, dreaming up options, and working on problems from different angles.

Although these managers didn't as yet set the strategies, they came to realize the attitudes necessary to do so. Strategies were guesses at the future by fallible human beings. "In financing an acquisition," one chief financial officer said, "financial models can eliminate the bad ways, but you're still left with five or so alternatives. There's no computer model that's going to predict the future for you. So finally, as always, it boils down to human judgment."

In learning about strategy, managers learned about business possibilities; but which business possibilities were viable depended on the culture of the corporation itself: its attitude toward risk and how it treated its employees. It was in seeing how the corporate culture operated that managers found out what was truly possible in their particular environment.

This understanding of what was possible was dominated by two factors: the nature of the company's business and the attitudes of the dominant people who ran it. A stable company in a stable business was unlikely to have a culture that encouraged heavy risks. A culture in which the norm was to talk everything over and get everyone's agreement before acting was not likely to be conducive to taking quick, decisive action. To succeed in any given culture, the managers had to learn to work within the norms and values of their organization.

From staff assignments, managers learned about strategy and culture and risk from firsthand exposure to how executives think about these issues. As with other developmental assignments, a year or two on the corporate staff helped managers make a mental transition, in this case from thinking tactically to thinking more strategically. They came to see a broader context in which decisions took place, and that one of the roles of an executive lay in constructing strategies for dealing with future events, then allowing others to carry out those strategies. (The lessons of staff assignments are summarized in figure 2–4.)

Individual Lessons

Setting and Implementing Agendas
- TECHNICAL/PROFESSIONAL SKILLS
- ALL ABOUT THE BUSINESS ONE IS IN
- STRATEGIC THINKING
- Shouldering full responsibility
- Building and using structure and control systems
- Innovative problem-solving methods

Handling Relationships
- Handling political situations
- Getting people to implement solutions
- WHAT EXECUTIVES ARE LIKE
- HOW TO WORK WITH EXECUTIVES
- Strategies of negotiation
- Dealing with people over whom you have no authority
- Understanding other people's perspectives
- Dealing with conflict
- Directing and motivating subordinates

Trial by Fire 41

- Developing other people
- Confronting subordinate performance problems
- Managing former bosses and peers

Basic Values
- You can't manage everything all alone
- Sensitivity to the human side of management
- Basic management values

Executive Temperament
- Being tough when necessary
- Self-confidence
- Coping with situations beyond your control
- Persevering through adversity
- **COPING WITH AMBIGUOUS SITUATIONS**
- Use (and abuse) of power

Personal Awareness
- The balance between work and personal life
- Knowing what really excites you about work
- Personal limits and blind spots
- Taking charge of your career
- Recognizing and seizing opportunities

Major Learning Thrusts

Understanding Corporate Strategies and Culture

Managers developed a broader technical framework within which to consider business possibilities and came to understand that the corporate culture also affected which possibilities were enacted.

Coping with an Ambiguous Situation

Managers learned to cope with their anxieties about dealing with powerful executives on topics where there could be no right answer and little that was tangible. They developed the attitudes necessary to take business risks consonant with an overall strategy.

See Lindsey, et al., *Key Events in Executives' Lives,* Technical Report No. 32 (Greensboro, N.C.: Center for Creative Leadership, 1987).

Figure 2–4. *The Potential Lessons of Line-to-Staff Switches*

Persuasion and Strategy

Projects and task forces and switches from line to staff jobs, if containing the core elements that demand learning the skills, could be the classroom for understanding business strategy and how to get things done when key people aren't on board. But in spite of these and the other lessons these experiences could teach, they aren't enough. Leading by persuasion is critical, but executives also have to use their authority, take full responsibility—in short, lead on line. The skills required for this kind of leadership weren't learned in the ambiguity and nonaccountability of staff jobs, the shared responsibility of a task force, or the singlemindedness of a project. Being in charge, as we have noted, does not mean that persuasion isn't critical. In fact, authority may mean little even when one has it. And strategic thinking is obviously important, even though the person in charge may face innumerable immediate demands and short-term pressures. Ultimately, the most successful executives will have the balance to handle both sides: to persuade and to use authority, to handle the here-and-now in ways that lead to a strategic future.

So, as important as they are, project/task force assignments and staff jobs are no substitute for challenging line experiences. As the next section will demonstrate, they don't make the same demands and they don't offer the same lessons.

Leading on Line: Full Responsibility

If projects, task forces, and staff assignments teach leadership by persuasion, developmental line assignments carry with them the lessons of power and accountability. Looking at what these executives had to do, one comes to understand why many of them are critical of people who "never had to make the bottom line." If persuasion-based assignments involved analytical distance, rubbing shoulders with executives several levels up, and coping with ambiguous, amorphous situations, the line leadership roles turned all the tables. These were down-and-dirty jobs, hands on,

Trial by Fire 43

action oriented, with real bottom lines, and sometimes involved managing casts of thousands.

Three major kinds of line assignments emerged as the firing line for leadership in the traditional taking-charge sense: starting something from scratch, turning a business around, and managing an operation of larger scope. Each type of assignment carried with it a somewhat different set of developmental implications, each offering its own special panoply of lessons. One kind of assignment, starting from scratch, offered the lessons of leadership in their purest form, as executives carved (sometimes literally) their mark on the world.

Starting from Scratch

> They offered me the job in South America, and let me know that if I took it they would fill in behind me and couldn't guarantee that I could ever come back to work for the company in the States. It's a little scary for a young man with two small children to do something like that. I didn't know if I'd like it over there, I'd never traveled outside the United States, and I was just a small-town boy. In fact, I didn't even tell my wife the part about maybe not coming back because she was already kind of panicky. Her father had come down to see me and wanted to know why I was taking his daughter and grandchildren out of the United States. Being a grandfather now, I can appreciate his opinion, but anyway, I did it.
>
> I went to Houston and spent three years designing the facility, which would end up being the world's largest offshore gas facility. Then I moved to Venezuela and we built it, and I ended up running it. I was 2,500 to 3,000 miles from a lot of help, making huge decisions without a lot of basis for making them. You just got all the facts you could and made 'em. At that age, twenty-eight or twenty-nine, making those kinds of decisions scared the hell out of you. Fortunately, most of them came out right.
>
> That place helped me learn to be at ease with making decisions. You learn to make decisions because you just have to make them. It wasn't that you were gifted in making decisions—you just didn't have anybody else to make them. Then later you had to go to your partners and justify what you were about. If you were

overspending your budget, you had to explain and tell them what you were doing about it. It's difficult to stand up in front of investors and say you're overspent, unless you can come up with a heck of a good story as to why. So you learn to make presentations, too.

The challenge of starting from scratch is easy to define: Build something from nothing. This something might include plants, product lines, new markets, or subsidiaries. In such start-up operations, managers may be plagued with all manner of adversities beyond the job itself: The managers we interviewed built towns in the wilderness, created policies, confronted social, political and cultural problems they initially knew nothing about, and coped with some of the harshest weather on Earth.

In the midst of this, they were usually loosely supervised. "I was sent overseas to create a new market for a product," one executive said, "given carte blanche and absolutely no guidance. I had to find an office, hire people, and build a market from scratch while I carved profit-and-loss responsibility for a core business."

Many of the developmental start-up assignments were out of the United States, leaving the managers geographically isolated and often viewed with suspicion by the local population. Sometimes they found themselves trying to build a staff from scratch, hiring inexperienced workers (who couldn't speak English), or trying to make an efficient team out of antagonistic, wary groups.

Other disadvantages were occasionally present as well. Sometimes the corporate office was skeptical of the new operation, or considered the business a secondary one. Sometimes the job carried a stigma: "An overseas assignment is a graveyard in this company."

The focus of the managerial challenge in starting-from-scratch assignments was almost singular: survival through individual leadership, an advanced course in how to stand alone. This and the sheer number of demands put a premium on individual initiative. The urgency, lack of structure, and frequent inexperience of the staff resulted in using whomever and whatever was available to solve problems. Strategies that would slow down progress weren't considered viable, no matter how sensible; any reflective pauses would come much later.

Four strong learning thrusts (see figure 2–5) stood out from scratch assignments:

- Out of chaos and demands, managers learned how to identify what was important and how to organize themselves to get it done.
- Creating a staff taught them how to select, train, and motivate subordinates.
- Living through the event successfully taught them they could survive. This raw endurance carried with it increased confidence and willingness to take risks.
- They learned firsthand how much leadership matters and how lonely the role can be.

Not all of the start-ups that executives described were as demanding as the Venezuelan gas plant. Instead of starting with absolutely nothing, some began with a facility, or more simply rolled out a new product. As the degree of challenge decreased, so too did the power of the lessons. At their toughest, start-ups were a pure jolt of adrenalin, described by one executive as "the purest time of my life." And, when the assignment was over, unlike many jobs they had held, the managers left behind something permanent, something they had created. For some managers, there would never be another job like it, and indeed some could never adjust to a job at corporate headquarters.

Fixing a Business in Trouble

Troubled operations, even disastrous ones, are commonplace in the business world: units rocked by fraud and scandal, teams that are the laughingstock of the company, groups with no financial controls, divisions that lose money year after year, and businesses whose profits plunge precipitously. Being sent in to "turn around" an operation—fix it!—was a frequently cited developmental experience.

Individual Lessons

Setting and Implementing Agendas
- Technical/professional skills
- ALL ABOUT THE BUSINESS ONE IS IN
- Strategic thinking
- SHOULDERING FULL RESPONSIBILITY
- Building and using structure and control systems
- Innovative problem-solving methods

Handling Relationships
- Handling political situations
- Getting people to implement solutions
- What executives are like
- How to work with executives
- Strategies of negotiation
- DEALING WITH PEOPLE OVER WHOM YOU HAVE NO AUTHORITY
- UNDERSTANDING OTHER PEOPLE'S PERSPECTIVES
- Dealing with conflict
- DIRECTING AND MOTIVATING SUBORDINATES
- Developing other people
- Confronting subordinate performance problems
- Managing former bosses and peers

Basic Values
- You can't manage everything all alone
- Sensitivity to the human side of management
- Basic management values

Executive Temperament
- Being tough when necessary
- Self-confidence
- Coping with situations beyond your control
- Persevering through adversity
- Coping with ambiguous situations
- Use (and abuse) of power

Personal Awareness
- The balance between work and personal life
- KNOWING WHAT REALLY EXCITES YOU ABOUT WORK

> - Personal limits and blind spots
> - Taking charge of your career
> - Recognizing and seizing opportunities
>
> *Major Learning Thrusts*
>
> - Out of chaos and demands, managers learned how to identify what's important and how to organize themselves to get it done.
> - Creating a staff taught them how to select, train, and motivate subordinates.
> - Living through the event successfully taught them "I could survive." This raw endurance carried with it increased confidence and willingness to take risks.
> - They learned firsthand how much leadership matters and how lonely the role can be.
>
> See Lindsey, et al., *Key Events in Executives' Lives,* Technical Report No. 32 (Greensboro, N.C.: Center for Creative Leadership, 1987), 7–20.

Figure 2–5. *The Potential Lessons of Starting from Scratch*

As reported by the managers we studied, the challenge of the assignment varied little: They were sent in to tear down and build back up systems and staff. The mandate was to reorganize, although no one knew exactly how to accomplish this. The reorganization often involved installing new systems (of financial or material controls, for example) that managers were unfamiliar with.

By definition, they faced serious staffing problems. Staff were demoralized, or unskilled, or lacked direction, or there was dissension among them. Sometimes the new manager had to deal with the legacy of the former boss as well.

Managers sent to turn things around usually had the formal authority they needed to carry out the mandate to fix it. One executive described how he used this authority to clean house:

> I inherited a financial function in total disarray. I had drunks and subordinates so abrasive that no internal client would work with

them. To turn it around, I fired a corporate officer, transferred people, retired others, and hired a combination of experienced outsiders and younger staff. Structurally, I appointed two lieutenants, one to run the function and another to handle administration. At the same time, I formed a study team and gave them six months to reorganize operations.

Perhaps surprisingly, not all fix-it managers had the authority to make the mandated changes. While it might seem cruel or at least foolish to send anyone into a fix-it with no authority to act, there are times when authority is useless, even destructive. Almost without exception, managers had the authority to act when the fix-it occurred in a single division or function, but they sometimes lacked formal authority when dealing with multiple divisions or functions as the result of a reorganization. As a result of a merger, for example, a manager might have to deal with several warring divisions or groups recently thrown together. One had to install a highly technical financial and administrative system when the divisions really didn't want them and where the management practices varied tremendously. "I had the authority to make people talk with each other," the executive recalled. "But getting them to work with each other when they never had and didn't figure they needed to? Where would I get that kind of authority and what good would it do? That job was a primer in the art of nudging."

Learning from developmentally potent fix-its came in two parallel thrusts: being tough and persuasive, and being tough and instrumental.

Tough and Persuasive.

> When I was a kid, I thought that most decisions were a matter of choosing right over wrong.... I'm still looking to make a decision like that. It seems that all my decisions are between two goods or two bads.

In fix-it assignments, managers must make tough decisions, decisions that will inevitably result in human pain. One manager we interviewed closed a plant in Iran during the 1979 revolution; another had to fire an entire department in fifteen-minute intervals. "It was kinder than letting people sweat it out for days until their turn came." His other choice was to change the operation against overwhelming resistance, or to let it wallow until most of those involved would have been fired or demoted anyway.

So managers had to be tough, but they needed to be persuasive at the same time. One manager who inherited an ailing financial function as part of a fix-it assignment was faced with the fact that the man who ran finance was not performing well. But he'd been with the company for forty years. He was a decent fellow whose skills had simply become obsolete. Did the manager dump him unceremoniously or give him a chance to save face? After some agonizing over this, the manager realized that just because a new financial system and new reporting relationship had been decreed didn't mean they were going to be implemented as written. *What* was going to happen was a given; how and with what degree of cooperation they would happen was up to the people involved. So even though it might have been so much easier to dismiss everyone who didn't seem to fit in, the truth was that he was going to have to work with people one way or another.

In coming to this realization, he seemed to have grasped the essence of the situation: that it was possible to tear something to bits without tearing up the people involved. He could explain what was going to happen and why, listen to their worries and fears, supply them with facts, and even concede that they might have a better idea. Although a few people might have to be dismissed, it was better to work with those you inherited. Many times, all they lacked was direction, control systems, and standards that made sense to them.

The ultimate lesson was straightforward. You can tear things down by decree, but building them back up is another matter. Authority isn't much help in getting people to work together. People need to believe they are moving toward something better, and that the change in the long run will be worth it. The managers learned that they had to live with their people once the changes were over.

Tough and Instrumental. The potential for developing a hard-boiled attitude toward people is the dark side of fix-it assignments. The pressure from upper management is immense, changes must be made, and the time managers have to fix operations is limited—six months to two years on average in our study. Sometimes, we found, it was necessary and sometimes simply easier to tell rather than consult, or to fire rather than to develop.

The managers we interviewed confronted fraud, gross negligence, abuses of sick leave and vacation, and widespread cheating on expense accounts. They inherited units millions of dollars in the red; they confronted hostile unions. Often their choice was between firing a few people or waffling until the ax fell on the entire group. Due to this, the assignment could be psychologically brutal. "Letting people go is never easy, no matter how justified." As their skins thickened, calluses could form over emotions as well.

Some managers began to focus narrowly on systems and standards and how to get people to do a job quickly. Rationalizing their actions was easy later, if the fix-it succeeded. They had saved jobs and turned a crummy division into an inspiring place to work. All the numbers looked good. Maybe they were promoted. But they paid a price for their success. Some, particularly those who became fix-it specialists, made themselves more or less immune to caring.

The essential tension of a fix-it (tear down and build back up) requires a certain oppositeness in a manager's behavior: a thick skin, on the one hand, to confront problems and take action; the ability to persuade and control, on the other, for dealing with groups over which they had no control or for situations where authority didn't matter. Unlike a start-up, where a manager could "do it right the first time," the turn-around required strategic pruning and making the best of what was left. "You can't replace a two of clubs with a four of clubs," one executive learned the hard way, discovering that it can be easier to fire people than to hire better ones. Some executives found fix-its so difficult to pull off that they tried to turn them into start-ups: "I would have loved to manage this place when it was brand new.

It is so much easier to put in the right processes when you start than it is to change the wrong processes to the right processes."

So a fix-it (see figure 2–6 for a summary of lessons) is quite different from a start-up, and both are different from managing a large operation that is doing basically okay, the topic of the next section.

A Leap in Scope

> Prior to that assignment, I was running a division of about $80 million a year in sales. This was a billion-dollar-a-year business. This was quite a jump for me, into a business that I knew absolutely nothing about. I didn't know the product. I didn't know the customers. I was terrified. Absolutely terrified.
>
> My boss's boss told me that I was running a new ship. He said what I ran before was a rowboat and this is the Queen Mary. In a rowboat, you make a little correction to the rudder and the boat immediately responds. The Queen Mary doesn't respond to the rudder as quickly. You have to have a lot of patience, or you'll make some big errors.

A leap in scope—from a rowboat to the Queen Mary—was developmental when it involved an increase in responsibility that was both broader and different from what has gone before. It was distinguished from either a start-up or a fix-it (which were sometimes large-scope jobs, too) in that the operation was doing basically okay, and the objective was to move it forward.

Executives in our study described scope changes of three basic kinds: promotions in the same function or area, promotions into new functions or areas, and lateral moves. Such moves could be massive (for example, being promoted two levels into a different business) or modest, but an increase in scope means a relative increase in the number of people, dollars, and functions to manage.

Learning from leaps in scope depended in part on the size of the change. The larger the leap, the more challenge the change presented and the greater the learning demands. Even a more modest shift, however, could teach some version of the basic

Individual Lessons

Setting and Implementing Agendas
- Technical/professional skills
- ALL ABOUT THE BUSINESS ONE IS IN
- Strategic thinking
- SHOULDERING FULL RESPONSIBILITY
- BUILDING AND USING STRUCTURE AND CONTROL SYSTEMS
- INNOVATIVE PROBLEM-SOLVING METHODS

Handling Relationships
- Handling political situations
- Getting people to implement solutions
- What executives are like
- How to work with executives
- STRATEGIES OF NEGOTIATION
- DEALING WITH PEOPLE OVER WHOM YOU HAVE NO AUTHORITY
- Understanding other people's perspectives
- Dealing with conflict
- DIRECTING AND MOTIVATING SUBORDINATES
- Developing other people
- CONFRONTING SUBORDINATE PERFORMANCE PROBLEMS
- MANAGING FORMER BOSSES AND PEERS

Basic Values
- You can't manage everything all alone
- Sensitivity to the human side of management
- Basic management values

Executive Temperament
- BEING TOUGH WHEN NECESSARY
- Self-confidence
- Coping with situations beyond your control
- PERSEVERING THROUGH ADVERSITY
- Coping with ambiguous situations
- Use (and abuse) of power

Personal Awareness
- The balance between work and personal life
- Knowing what really excites you about work

Trial by Fire

> - Personal limits and blind spots
> - Taking charge of your career
> - Recognizing and seizing opportunities
>
> *Major Learning Thrusts*
>
> *Being Tough and Persuasive*
> Managers learned to make tough decisions when whichever way they turned there was a human cost. They also learned that the best way to tear something down and build it back up was to get others committed to the changes.
>
> *Being Tough and Instrumental*
> Some managers focused on the task at hand and made changes by the numbers rather than through people. While in disastrous situations this was sometimes called for, often their lack of caring was counterproductive.
>
> Fix-it assignments teach toughness and how to set up structure and control systems needed to turn businesses around. Managers were most often persuasive when they had to be; when they had full authority, they were more often instrumental in their treatment of others.
>
> See Esther Lindsey, et al., *Key Events in Executives' Lives,* Technical Report No. 32 (Greensboro, N.C.: Center for Creative Leadership, 1987), 21–40.

Figure 2–6. *The Potential Lessons of Fix-Its*

learning thrusts: learning to develop subordinates and learning to think like an executive.

Learning to Develop Subordinates. Executives may say they know how to delegate, but it wasn't until they faced a job that was much too big for them to handle alone that many of them discovered what that really meant. Like any other adult learner, they learned something when they needed to, and it was overwhelming scope that taught some executives that they "couldn't manage it all alone." Only when the managers had total responsibility ("I was in charge of everything corporatewide") did much purposeful development of others take place. There wasn't any choice.

But the problem was greater than this. In addition to developing people that the managers could trust to run the operation for them, they also faced the issue of creating a challenging climate where people had the room and the resources to continue developing. To do this, the managers had to make sure people knew the strategy behind the specifics so that they knew what was expected of them and why. "If you expect 15 percent growth, tell them why that number was chosen," one said. These successful managers shared information across units and functions, even information that their subordinates seemingly didn't need to know to do their jobs. Who were they to say what connections, what ideas, what ramifications might result from sharing the strategy?

Learning to Think Like an Executive. Because they couldn't keep their arms around it all and *had* to let others run things, the managers had to behave differently than they had in previous jobs. They had to tolerate mistakes and efficiency that was perhaps 90 percent of what they thought it should be. Increasingly, they had to learn to "manage by remote control"—staying informed, prodding, pushing, asking lots of questions, but not doing. Much of their job became clearing the way so their people could get their work done—supplying information and money and buffering them from interference.

Responsibility was theirs as always, although it took on a different form. Responsibility for doing the job was replaced with responsibility for seeing that systems and work processes were set up so that it got done. Their control over what was done lay in their ability to figure out what was important.

Most of the managers used cliches and catchphrases to symbolize what they thought was important, but the best of them actually lived those catchphrases. If they believed in "close to the customer," they spent lots of time with customers; if they raved about quality, they were willing to pay for it and to change practices to make it better. If costs were a problem, they didn't fly off to faraway resorts in the corporate jet. As their role became increasingly symbolic, they learned that being closely watched by corporate staff was nothing compared with being closely watched by *everyone* in their operation. Did they talk about caring and never thank their secretary? Did they trumpet innovation and dump all over new ideas? Did they herald aggressiveness and fold the first time someone threatened a lawsuit?

Congruence was important. Consistency was important. Setting astronomical goals and then driving themselves and everyone else toward them was important. Their people didn't expect them to be omniscient, nor to do it all, but they did expect them to lead, to push indefatigably, and to be out there showing some guts.

Nothing could be further from the executive's life than the serene boardrooms and barren, polished desks often portrayed in the media. Over forty studies of managerial work dating back to the 1950s have shown that "executives just sort of dash around all the time." Executives work on many problems simultaneously, endure numerous interruptions, and manage hundreds of contacts who weave in and out on a regular basis. Little time is spent giving orders; more often the job is one of juggling problems and cajoling others as a series of events streams by. Executives may go from a discussion of a billion-dollar capital investment to a customer complaint to taking care of a broken copier in the space of minutes.[21] The managers we studied knew that controlling their time or the problems that appeared was something they could direct only up to a point.

With increasing scope, executives had to learn to be comfortable with events running without them. They could prod, insist, structure, emphasize the importance of a few priorities, tear apart faulty logic, and see what happened. They had gotten where they were by relying on themselves; now, as shown in figure 2–7, they were learning how to rely on, develop, and manage the stuff of others. This is no small transition.

Leading on Line

The three kinds of assignments, all quite different, have in common the demand that the leader be in charge, unlike events that

Individual Lessons

Setting and Implementing Agendas
- Technical/professional skills
- All about the business one is in
- Strategic thinking
- Shouldering full responsibility
- **BUILDING AND USING STRUCTURE AND CONTROL SYSTEMS**
- Innovative problem-solving methods

Handling Relationships
- Handling political situations
- **GETTING PEOPLE TO IMPLEMENT SOLUTIONS**
- What executives are like
- How to work with executives
- Strategies of negotiation
- Dealing with people over whom you have no authority
- Understanding other people's perspectives
- Dealing with conflict
- **DIRECTING AND MOTIVATING SUBORDINATES**
- **DEVELOPING OTHER PEOPLE**
- Confronting subordinate performance problems
- **MANAGING FORMER BOSSES AND PEERS**

Basic Values
- **YOU CAN'T MANAGE EVERYTHING ALL ALONE**
- Sensitivity to the human side of management
- Basic management values

Executive Temperament
- Being tough when necessary
- Self-confidence
- Coping with situations beyond your control
- Persevering through adversity
- Coping with ambiguous situations
- Use (and abuse) of power

Personal Awareness
- The balance between work and personal life
- Knowing what really excites you about work
- Personal limits and blind spots

Trial by Fire

> - Taking charge of your career
> - Recognizing and seizing opportunities
>
> *Major Learning Thrusts*
>
> *Relying on Other People*
> Because the job had grown so large, managers felt compelled to do more than direct and motivate others to accomplish tasks that they set—they had to develop their people so they could determine the *what* for themselves.
>
> *Thinking Like an Executive*
> Managers made a mental transition—from doing things well to seeing that they were done well.
>
> See Esther Lindsey, et al., *Key Events in Executives' Lives,* Technical Report No. 32 (Greensboro, N.C.: Center for Creative Leadership, 1987), 55–69.

Figure 2–7. *The Potential Lessons of Scope*

teach leading through persuasion. Starting from scratch, turning a business around, and big-scope jobs all emphasize standing alone, making the decisions, taking responsibility. In short, the leader is accountable, not only for his or her own actions but also for the actions of those working for him and for the business outcomes (the bottom line).

With this accountability come varying degrees of authority, sometimes absolute authority. Learning how to use power and when to use it are the major challenges of line jobs like these.

An Overview of Developmental Assignments

There are many long-forgotten jobs in a career. It may be true that something can be learned in any job, but across more than three hundred developmental assignments described for this research, no executive mentioned going into a stable, predictable business loaded down with policies or directives as being a major learning event. It was rare to hear about serving on a task force on some marginal topic—revamping a performance appraisal form, for example. Job changes that involved staying with exactly the same people or doing a job that was familiar, or where it was impossible to know how well they did, were rarely mentioned as well. By their absence, we can conclude that low-risk job changes seldom generated lasting change as far as these executives were concerned.

Even the moderately risky and common practices of laterally transferring young managers or promoting them in the same unit were seldom described as turning-point jobs after the early work years. Job rotations per se—such as switching from one marketing role to another in a different division, brief exposure stints in different functions, or simple promotions such as going from plant controller in a small operation to plant controller in a larger one—go only part of the way toward being truly developmental. Even though such moves might offer exposure to new business topics, or different people or groups or products to worry about, they are essentially more of the same.

It would seem that neither exposure without accountability nor small increases in responsibility are as valuable developmentally as diversity in the types of assignments. They don't offer what is most important in development—jobs that demand dealing with sudden, unexpected changes or that call for skills the manager doesn't have. The essence of development is that diversity and adversity beat repetition every time. The more dramatic the change in skill demands, the more severe the personnel problems, the more the bottom line pressure, and the more sinuous and unexpected the turns in the road, the more opportunity there is for learning. Unappealing as they may seem, being shocked and pressured and having problems with other people teach most. For future executives, comfortable circumstances are hardly the road to the top.

The Core Elements of Developmental Assignments

As we mentioned at the beginning of this chapter, these particular five assignments were especially developmental because of

Trial by Fire 59

the challenges—the core elements—they contained. To succeed at them, managers *had* to learn. They had to learn new skills on the run, learn to act when the stakes were high, learn to work with trying people under trying circumstances, and learn to cope with an exhausting workload. They developed because they had to.

New Skills on the Run. These five kinds of assignments presented managers with situations in which old skills no longer served. Lacking the necessary knowledge, experience, background, or skills was so commonplace in these assignments that it can be considered a developmental prerequisite. What varied was how big the deficit was, usually somewhere between moderate and massive. It might not have been so difficult if all the manager had to do was finesse the missing trumps. What put the thrill in it was having to make up for the gaps while at the same time progressing against the core challenge of the job—keeping the business afloat long enough to fix it, for example.

Play for High Stakes. All five types of developmental assignments were high pressure; the stakes for which the managers were playing were often enormous. They were given profit-and-loss responsibility in multimillion-dollar operations; they worked on projects where their recommendations could affect the future of the business; without formal authority, they were made responsible for coordinating multiple, warring functions that were geographically dispersed; they inherited businesses in deep financial trouble; or they were thrown in to build a specific function during the chaos of a total reorganization. Because of this kind of pressure, these five types of assignments were often a pure test. Top management put in the best people they had and then peered over their shoulders to see how they were doing.

Trying People, Trying Times. These assignments demanded working with people under difficult circumstances. The assignments brought managers into direct conflict with many groups that were unfamiliar to them, including foreign governments, unions, and joint venture partners. Managers ended up demoting people, firing people, and installing systems and procedures that employees resisted, all of which demanded the utmost of their interpersonal skills.

One manager said he "was as welcome as a skunk in church" as he tried to get plants in seven different countries to cooperate. Another told a tale of having the rug pulled out from under him as well:

> While on a special assignment modernizing and computerizing the process in a plant, I had to deal simultaneously with lots of problem workers I'd inherited. There were raging personality conflicts, incompetent folks, and I was also overseeing my former boss and some of my former peers. After really pitching in to face those problems head on, I was told to carry out a staff reduction because of lagging profit, and according to union rules, seniority was the criterion for retention. All that effort to improve skills and relationships, and the years of service was all that mattered.
>
> I let them go, picked myself up, and started over, rebuilding their confidence, listening to the workers' fears and trying to instill pride of ownership in what must have seemed an arbitrary world to them.

Handle the Physical Strain. These assignments were usually physically and mentally exhausting. The unrelenting pace, the long hours, and the travel took a toll on the manager. "I worked 365 days the first year," one manager said. (He had just taken charge of a subsidiary that everyone had warned him was a "tar baby.") "The subsidiary had no human resources function for over 4,000 people, a horrible reputation for being secretive and uncooperative, and chronic union problems." Such nonstop problems made some managers merely jittery, and created in others profound frustration. The jobs that made a difference were as draining as they were exciting.

Learning from Assignments

Figures 2–8 and 2–9 summarize the lessons executives said they took from stage-setting early work experiences and from the five

Developmental Assignments	Learning Thrusts
Early Work Experience	Transition to work
	People at work
	Insight into self
First Supervisory Experience	Management is different from technical work
Project/Task Force	Giving up technical mastery
	Understanding other people's points of view
Line-to-Staff Switches	Coping with an ambiguous situation
	Understanding corporate strategies and culture
Starting Something from Scratch	Identifying what's important
	Building a team
	Surviving tough situations
	How leadership matters
Fix-It/Turnaround Jobs	Being tough and persuasive
	Being tough and instrumental
Leaps in Scope	Relying on other people
	Thinking like an executive

Figure 2–8. *Potential Learning from Assignments*

major assignments. It's an impressive list, a veritable encyclopedia of executive education. As we will show, it's not the whole story, but it's clear that challenging assignments were major sources of learning for the executives we studied.

Seeing these results in list form tempts us to think of development in dangerously oversimplified ways. Why not program executive development: After they've supervised a while, they'll be assigned to a task force, then sent to start something, next a year at corporate staff, then a big-scope line job, and finally a fix-it caper. There are some good reasons why such an approach can-

Setting and Implementing Agendas
- TECHNICAL/PROFESSIONAL SKILLS
- ALL ABOUT THE BUSINESS ONE IS IN
- STRATEGIC THINKING
- SHOULDERING FULL RESPONSIBILITY
- BUILDING AND USING STRUCTURE AND CONTROL SYSTEMS
- INNOVATIVE PROBLEM-SOLVING METHODS

Handling Relationships
- HANDLING POLITICAL SITUATIONS
- GETTING PEOPLE TO IMPLEMENT SOLUTIONS
- WHAT EXECUTIVES ARE LIKE
- HOW TO WORK WITH EXECUTIVES
- STRATEGIES OF NEGOTIATION
- DEALING WITH PEOPLE OVER WHOM YOU HAVE NO AUTHORITY
- UNDERSTANDING OTHER PEOPLE'S PERSPECTIVES
- DEALING WITH CONFLICT
- DIRECTING AND MOTIVATING SUBORDINATES
- DEVELOPING OTHER PEOPLE
- CONFRONTING SUBORDINATE PERFORMANCE PROBLEMS
- MANAGING FORMER BOSSES AND PEERS

Basic Values
- YOU CAN'T MANAGE EVERYTHING ALL ALONE
- SENSITIVITY TO THE HUMAN SIDE OF MANAGEMENT
- Basic management values

Executive Temperament
- BEING TOUGH WHEN NECESSARY
- SELF-CONFIDENCE
- Coping with situations beyond your control
- PERSEVERING THROUGH ADVERSITY
- COPING WITH AMBIGUOUS SITUATIONS
- Use (and abuse) of power

Personal Awareness
- The balance between work and personal life
- KNOWING WHAT REALLY EXCITES YOU ABOUT WORK
- Personal limits and blind spots
- Taking charge of your career
- Recognizing and seizing opportunities

See Lindsey, et al., *Key Events in Executives' Lives,* Technical Report No. 32 (Greensboro, N.C.: Center for Creative Leadership, 1987).

Figure 2-9. *The Potential Lessons of Assignments*

not work, and in fact, lockstep approaches run counter to everything we learned about how these successful executives developed. Making effective use of developmental assignments requires an understanding of *how* these executives learned from assignments and of the imbalances that learning from assignments can create.

How These Executives Learned. In general, adults learn when they need to or have to, and these executives were no exception. Because of the demanding nature of these assignments, learning was not a nicety—something to be done out of interest or because it might be helpful. Learning was something these managers did because they had little choice but to take action—stab at problems even if they weren't sure what they were doing, because doing nothing was surely unacceptable. They did quick studies on unfamiliar topics, tried something, and learned from how it came out. They learned where they could when they could from whom they could.

The lessons stuck because they were the result of things these managers did, not things they watched others do. When they succeeded, their mark was left on a plant or an operational system. They had overcome many obstacles to leave that mark, and taken risks, so the learning was tied to their own success. Sometimes taking risks and winning became addictive. One executive, who had drilled for oil in a rain forest, put it this way: "That was the purest time of my life. No offices, no memos. Conditions were horrible, but oh, it was exciting. I can't describe the exhilaration of that time."

Learning because you have to in order to succeed, and having that learning reinforced by success, made assignments potent teachers. But such dynamics are very difficult to manipulate—and people are quick to detect when someone else is pulling the strings. These executives were playing for keeps, and that was critical to the learning process. Bosses, the organization, and human resource people might give advice or put up safety nets behind the scenes, but the learning had to be on line. As we will see later, keeping the assignments "real" is essential to making use of experience for development.

Imbalances from Assignments.

> We should be careful to get out of an experience only the wisdom that is in it—and stop there; lest we be like the cat that sits down on a hot stove lid. She will never sit down on a hot stove lid again—and that is well; but also she will never sit down on a cold one anymore.
> —Mark Twain

The danger of assignments is not, like the cat in *Pudd'nhead Wilson,* that managers will avoid hot stove lids. The danger is that they will believe hot stove lids are all there is. For assignments are so gripping, so stressful—and succeeding at them so satisfying—that the action itself becomes addictive. As John Kotter noted in his study of general managers, "Because [they] were so successful, because they often had twenty- or thirty-year track records of win after win, many seemed to have developed an attitude of 'I can do anything.'"[22]

If management success were a tally sheet, where one checked off this skill or that assignment once it was mastered, assignments would be enough. But as developmentally rich as they are, assignments can take a budding executive only part of the way. There are three potential downsides to assignments:

- They emphasize personal confidence at the expense of realizing one's limits and weak spots, which can lead to arrogance.
- They emphasize toughness at the expense of sensitivity to others, which can lead to using people as instruments.
- They emphasize independence at the expense of acquiring a developmental perspective, which can lead to overmanaging.

Although none of the above are inevitable, they are potential sources of imbalance. As such, succeeding at assignments makes it easier to develop confidence in what one can do rather than what one can't; easier to learn how to get people to do a job rather than to care much about how to treat them as people, and easier to be an individual contributor than to reflect much on one's responsibilities as a manager.

From successful assignments, some executives do develop

confidence yet know their limits, and are tough yet sensitive to others. But like the other lessons of adulthood, the lessons of humility and compassion are learned most often when they have to be learned, and for success at assignments they are less often critical. Managers usually learn about their limits and weak spots when they are confronted with them—from making major business mistakes, from demotions and missed promotions, or when their family life falls apart. They most often learn about compassionate treatment of others and matters of integrity when they are done unto themselves—when an assortment of admirable and loutish people demonstrate those values (or lack of them) in action. So the lessons that come from what one accomplishes and what one does to and for others are different from the lessons that result from failure and being done unto by others.

In the next chapter, we'll explore a very different kind of experience that, according to these executives, led to lasting change. Instead of describing an assignment and what they faced, they described another person—almost always a boss—who had a lasting impact on them. What they learned from these very special bosses, and how they learned it, was quite different from successful assignments.

3
When Other People Matter

Assignments teach managers that they *must* learn to deal with all kinds of people. There simply is no choice; getting the job done is impossible without it. Like the need to grasp quickly new business or technical content, each new assignment requires sizing up and dealing with all the people entangled in it. In this sense, what managers learn about other people from assignments is predominantly instrumental. In pursuit of a goal, a manager must orchestrate the activities of others, using them as resources when they are moving in the same direction and treating them as problems to be solved when they are obstacles. From assignments, managers learn to persuade, cajole, "sell," direct, negotiate, and get tough, because these skills are essential. Success depends on it, failure is assured without it. The best plan ever devised is worthless if the boss pulls the rug out. The most brilliant strategy is only an abstraction if no one will carry it out.

But not all learning about other people comes from assignments. Almost 20 percent of the key events in the careers of the executives we studied featured a specific person rather than an assignment. At the center of these events were people who had a significant impact in their own right, far more important than the assignment at the time. These were the stories of individuals who, because of their position, or what they stood for, or what they did, left a vivid and lasting mark on the developing executive. They overshadowed the challenges of the assignment and other events facing the executive at the time. It was these people, not the business matters at hand, that were the force behind the learning in these key events.

It turns out that most of these people—fully 90 percent—were organizational superiors. One immediately thinks of the folklore on mentoring, which suggests that these relationships with a boss would have been long-term affairs in which the boss counseled and coached the "student" manager. Yet we found that the significant contacts with bosses from which enduring lessons were learned sometimes lasted only a few minutes and seldom longer than a few years. In his book *The Seasons of a Man's Life,* Levinson concluded that while intense mentoring relationships are important in adult development, they rarely occur on the job.[1]

But if a long-term mentoring relationship was not at the heart of the learning, why were bosses so often mentioned as sources of significant lessons? Why not peers or subordinates or friends? In fact, people other than bosses did play a role in executive learning. Executives reported learning from subordinates, for example, by successfully leading them (particularly in big-scope assignments and while starting businesses from scratch), by directly trying out new (for them) methods of directing and motivating them, and by having to confront them (a common feature in fix-it assignments and in hardships). But when executives learned from their subordinates, it was largely from the part subordinates played in a larger scenario and largely from how the subordinates reacted to the manager's own actions. In no case was a subordinate singled out, as bosses were, as a primary role model.

Similarly, executives learned to understand and work with peers as they took on various assignments (particularly task forces, which often required a group of peers to work together) or as they experienced a failure as a result of not taking peers into account. They also learned from watching what happens to their peers—usually through the actions of a boss. Peers also assumed a prominent role when executives attended external courses—they became the yardsticks against which managers measured themselves. But again, it was extremely rare for an executive to describe a key event centered primarily on a peer. Like subordinates, peers are usually important for the part they play in a larger context.

And so it goes with other important people in these executives' lives. External people were important parts of negotiations and of cross-cultural assignments. Wives, fathers, teachers, and coaches only occasionally appeared as major role models.

Most of the time, then, when another person was a significant learning event, that person was a boss. And with good reason. Bosses, after all, have the authority to affect directly the daily lives and often the career advancement of those who work for them. In *The Human Side of Enterprise,* McGregor goes so far as to suggest that every encounter with one's boss reinforces or modifies the attitudes, habits, or expectations of a subordinate.[2] Though this may be true, the question here is whether or not such encounters lead to lasting change. In those terms, not all bosses reported on by the executives we questioned were significant. Some left little or no lasting mark. Some were important only because they were part of an important assignment. (This was particularly true in the first management job and in assignments featuring a large change in scope.) But certain bosses—far more than any other type of person—left a permanent impression on the development of the managers we studied. These special bosses became events in and of themselves.

Three Types of Special Boss

Some of these long-remembered events involving bosses lasted only a moment, as we have said. Others played out over a period of years. Some involved the executive we interviewed directly, while others involved a boss's actions toward others. Regardless, the key to the importance of the event lay in its emotional impact. Perhaps it is the high emotional charge of these memories that led our executives to describe these special bosses in simple, black-and-white terms: They were good, they were bad, or they were some of both.

The majority of people who mattered most to the executives we studied were bosses who were remembered fondly—the good bosses—yet no single quality made all of the good bosses remarkable. Some of these bosses gave managers enough rope to try things on their own; some gave visibility and recognition; some were veritable geniuses in some aspect of business or in a technical area. Others were warm, supportive, and encouraging; still others were wise and dispensed counsel. There were those who opened doors for their people, and those who buffered their people from the vicissitudes of organizational life. Some gave their subordinates honest and straightforward appraisals, some provided insight into the personalities and politics of the organization, and some simply delegated exciting and challenging tasks.

In short, some of the "good" bosses were warm, and some were not. Some cared about their subordinates, some didn't. Some taught, some were oblivious to any teaching role. But they all had something positive to offer that the subordinate admired or needed. Whether it was to have a shot at the big time, or the room to make mistakes, or support and encouragement, or even the bitter medicine of honest criticism, these bosses played a pivotal role in the development of the manager below them. Sometimes it was pivotal not just because the boss was remarkable in one way or another but also because the relationship with the developing manager was one of support and closeness.

The picture changes abruptly as we consider the darker side of bosses. One third of these significant bosses were remembered as having few redeeming virtues. In these situations, managers not only saw actions and their impact but had to cope with a difficult relationship as well. Reflecting the emotional impact of these situations, executives were "appalled" at bosses they described as "pompous," "pigheaded," "dictatorial," "vindictive"; bosses who "raked people across the coals in front of a group" or who battered others with their intelligence. Equally compelling to the managers watching these role models were the reactions of others: sabotage, anger, mistrust, bitterness, and, above all, the anguish generated by cruelty. What they took away from these experiences were potent lessons in what *not* to do.

A few of the special bosses were described as amalgams of the good and the bad, with their greatest strength camouflaging an Achilles heel. "He gave lots of credit and made me very visible," an executive told us. "He dealt well with subordinates. He liked change and made you feel important if he liked you. But he was terrible with peers and bosses. He failed because he was too smart—he made other people feel stupid by always having to prove his intelligence."

More so than with either the good or the bad bosses, the impact of the flawed bosses was heightened by special, personal relationships with the subordinate. Some of the executives we interviewed remembered a "heart of gold" beneath the boss's crusty surface; others noted that this boss treated them differently from other subordinates: "I was the exception," one told us. The bond was sometimes identification: "I was like him"; sometimes pity: "It was such a waste of talent"; sometimes the respect that can come from "fighting like cats and dogs"; sometimes gratitude for opening doors or demanding excellence.

Exposure to these flawed bosses is, perhaps, the deepest learning opportunity offered by other people. Like the good bosses, they have a plethora of remarkable attributes that a developing manager might emulate. Like the bad, they are a demonstration of what should *not* be done. But the emergence of the flaw within the strength may be the important lesson: A talented, successful manager sees firsthand how another talented, successful manager can do himself in. It can be a first insight into the dynamics of derailment, showing how every strength is also a weakness; how blind spots matter, even when overshadowed by brilliance. "I knew," one said, "that I was like him. If I didn't do something about it, all my brilliant schemes would amount to nothing. It's easy when you're smart to lose your patience with others, but when you need them, they won't be there."

Learning from Bosses

Because these bosses—good, bad, or a mixture—made an impact through their special attributes, or their special liabilities, or because of the relationships they formed with subordinates, a variety of lessons could be learned from them. But the lessons of bosses were idiosyncratic—they depended on the boss. For this reason, most of the executives we interviewed were more likely to learn these lessons from some other source. A developing executive *might* learn just about anything from the "right boss at the right time." It appears to have been a hit-or-miss proposition.

Does this mean that exposure to significant other people doesn't matter? Absolutely not. They can be critical to executive learning for three major reasons.

First, they are sometimes a partial substitute for direct experience, teaching lessons an executive may otherwise have missed, simply because there are limits on how much a person can experience directly. Sometimes there aren't enough big-time assignments to go around, and even when there are, careers aren't long enough to do everything. There is consolation, then, that vicarious experience sometimes fills the gaps. Many of the lessons that assignments might teach can be gleaned from the right person at the right time. From bosses who were good at marketing, or strategy, or building teams, aspiring executives could learn different approaches to doing those things.

This is the kind of modeling influence, especially with regard to how to treat subordinates, that Marshall and Stewart found in their research.[3] Seeing others do it right, do it wrong, or do themselves in with a flaw underlying a remarkable talent, some executives learned that there are many ways to manage. So, other people can be important substitutes for, or complements to, direct experience. What a manager might not learn somewhere else, for lack of opportunity or just missing it the first time, might be learned from another person.

Second, bosses can teach some lessons that assignments can't teach at all, or in the same way. Managers and executives constantly face tough decisions where the interests of the business and the well-being of individuals clash. What is the humane way to close down a plant? At what point is there a moral obligation to refuse a boss's directive? How does one balance personal feelings toward individuals with the authority to influence their compensation and career? Assignments teach the courage and necessity to act in such situations, but it is primarily from bosses that executives form the values that guide their actions as managers and as people in an organizational setting.

Third, the lessons to be learned from bosses can be a very important balance to the lessons learned from assignments. Successful executives are individualistic, aggressive adults who are tempered by the challenge of a job to be done. Their success has been contingent on their ability to get other people to do what they want done; to get other people to help them, or get out of the way. Where does the countervailing force come from that offsets the insensitivity bred by this instrumental use of others? Where do the values come from that channel the use of power? The answer is, at least in part, that values are honed by significant other people, especially bosses, who, by virtue of who they are and what they do, profoundly affect successful managers.

And yet, good teachers are as rare in the corporation as they are in the rest of life. In his study of subordinate–boss relationships, Clawson found that the best bosses-as-teachers were those who made themselves available to subordinates, challenged subordinates with high standards, and managed to make the whole relationship a developmental experience.[4] Waiting for such a boss to turn up, believing that someone will "teach" you how to be a successful executive, is a mistake. Just as diversity in types of assignments is critical to growth, diversity in exposure to bosses is a key to development. But—and it's a big "but"—the successful executives we studied took responsibility for their own learning. Instead of denying critical feedback that hurt, they swallowed their pride and took it to heart. Instead of blaming everything on an intolerable boss, they dug out messages about themselves. Instead of dismissing other people because they were too old or too young or too abrasive or too soft or too different, they adopted the attitude that you can learn something from everyone. They seemed to realize that warm and supportive bosses didn't always tell you what you needed to hear, and they recognized that all people are blends of strengths and weaknesses. Not only can we learn from the strengths but also from the frailties. The lessons from other people are there for the taking, but, more often than not, a person must go after them.

Lessons from Bosses: The Good

One particularly exemplary boss we interviewed[5] did three things that had a significant impact on how his subordinates viewed the management job. The first involved his handling of a problem in relations with the union.

On his first day of work in his new job, the union went on strike. Ten thousand people walked. Gene, the boss in question, called a meeting with the union. Before the meeting, his industrial relations manager pulled him aside and told him he (Gene) didn't understand these people. They were like animals; they were brutal. "There are two topics you never talk about," he said, "nonunion plants in the South and subcontracting." Gene didn't respond. He walked in and said: "You fellows didn't have to pull that show of power. I knew you were in charge. All you did was waste a lot of people's pay. Now the first meeting is going to be brief, so we're only going to discuss two subjects: nonunion plants in the South and subcontracting."

After that, he gave a speech to his managers about getting on better with the unions. He got no response at first, but he stuck to his plan. For example, at negotiations the union representative would always sit at one end of a long table and raise his voice to speak to the management representative at the other end. Gene simply moved his chair right beside the union man, figuring the two of them were more likely to speak quietly at that distance. Later, he discovered that the union had bugged his office, but he left the device in place. "I want them to know what I go through," he explained. "Besides, I'm going to tell them everything anyway. I'm going to give them the same reports I give to management." Over a period of time, what had been a bad relationship began to be much more constructive. Gene had taken the tension out of the situation.

The second thing this particular boss did involved customer relations. Again this had an important effect on his subordinates. While Gene was on a business trip, one of the turbines manufactured by his division failed at a plant nearby. Gene went right down and stayed until the problem was solved. When he returned, he told his key subordinates that he was going to visit every failure and give a personal report to the executives of that utility. His subordinates advised against doing so. He would never have the time to do it. One subordinate even told Gene that the engineers were angry, thinking he was doing their job. Gene just smiled and said, "There's nothing more important," and visited every failure for the next two years.

The final story has to do with this boss's attitude toward involvement and participation. Shortly after Gene took over, he persuaded the board to consolidate two formerly separate operations at the new site. He appointed ninety engineers to conduct site studies and to design the new plant. It took years, and many of the engineers were against it from the beginning. Gene firmly repeated his only ground rules on the project: "We're moving" and "You can spend $60 million to build this plant." Gradually the engineers began to look forward to their meetings with him. They would argue, break into small groups, then argue some more. Slowly they began to catch his vision of something beautiful, a state-of-the-art facility. When the consolidated plant opened, boasting technology only dreamed of before, morale was sky-high, as there were essentially no customer complaints. But Gene had one more trick up his sleeve. Before building the plant, he had purchased acreage near the site. After construction, he sold this land. That and the productivity improvements more than offset the cost of the land, the building, and the move. Gene managed in the end to build a sixty-million-dollar facility for nothing.

These are examples of how the actions of a good boss can shape the attitudes of subordinates. It matters little whether Gene's actions were consciously symbolic or simply actions in service of his business vision. What mattered was that he exemplified in his actions a consistent set of values. What his subordinates learned came from watching an exemplary boss.

The union problem showed that open communication was a value that could pay off: Gene treated the union the same way he treated any other employees, telling them what he was doing and why, and involving them in the decisions.

By visiting every product failure, he showed the customers (and his employees) what it meant to provide quality and service.

A concrete example of how the value of customer service could pay off came on the handling of lawsuits from customers. Gene put together a booklet of information to those same customers, telling them what all the problems with the turbines were (over the chief counsel's howls of protest), and offered them discounted services to correct them. They accepted, dropped the lawsuits, and joined with the company in correcting the problems. Not a penny changed hands.

When he created a task force of engineers for two years to build the new plant, he demonstrated two things: that he trusted them to make the highest quality decisions, and that they could in fact influence events.

This example illustrates one of the most common learning themes from bosses: that one's values are reflected in one's actions. From good bosses, subordinates could see that integrity, trust, compassion, and other "abstract" values could make a difference.

In learning from good bosses, subordinates tended to note whatever the boss was good at: If bosses gave rope, subordinates came to grips with what it meant to have autonomy; if bosses were brilliant at motivating subordinates, subordinates tried to model this in their own behavior; if they shone with integrity, subordinates tried to figure out what their own actions said about themselves. Whatever their special strengths, good bosses played a central role in the education of these future executives: as coaches, as structurers of their jobs, and as the personification of values.

Lessons from Bosses: The Bad[6]

For every two bosses described as being good, executives described one they perceived as being bad.

One boss, for example, kept a dossier on everyone he knew well and wouldn't hesitate to use it. One played a ruthless game in which he would bring up a seemingly insurmountable problem and then disparage every solution his subordinates proposed. When they ran out of ideas, he would present them with the solution he had in mind all along. In contrast, some bad bosses shirked their responsibilities, seemingly unable or unwilling to make decisions.

Gene (the exemplary boss in the preceding example) himself had a boss who ruled by terror.

> Before I was a manager, I worked in a division that only had one customer, the military, so our real boss was the military manager. The first time I saw him, he brought in a team of experts to grill one of my associates. About ten minutes into it, he screamed: "Why don't you sit down and get someone up there that knows what the hell they're talking about!" I got tapped and, mercifully, it went OK.
>
> There are numerous horror stories about this guy, how he browbeat people, ruined careers and so forth, but he taught me some lessons:
>
> First, he questioned everything and was often right. I hate detail, but he made me attend to it. I'm unsure I could have handled the later plant consolidation without that object lesson.
>
> Second, I learned how to cope with irrational reactions. I figured he wanted me in the job and wouldn't have me removed, and I figured that the facts are always your best bet. Years later, I used that tactic with the opposition to the new plant. Other executives wanted the money for their own operations, so I destroyed their arguments by showing the net cost to be zero. They looked silly arguing against it. With him, I showed him the numbers and told him I wasn't going to make a product at a loss.
>
> Third, I learned that there are lots of ways to get results, not just mine. He came into my office one day and told me that the product was perfect, that he had nothing to complain about. I grinned and said, "Hey, there's a lot of people out there waiting for you." He said, "Yes, I suppose you're right" and went in there bellowing, "When are you idiots going to get it right?"
>
> So his behavior was partly an act, but he did some hard things as well. If you look under the surface, try to understand people, you can usually find some common ground. He was a perfectionist who considered any defect in a product a threat to national security. He believed he was doing the right thing.
>
> He was also a great model of what not to do. His strategy was a short-term one that may work if you hold all the cards. To inspire people, to get them committed, you do the opposite.

Gene's experience and the lessons he learned from it reflect the experience of many executives who, at some point, found themselves at the mercy of a boss with few redeeming qualities. Unable to immediately extricate themselves from the situation, they were left with little choice but to find a way to make the relationship work: understanding your adversary, coping with what he threw at you, and learning what *not* to do.

While one might expect to learn compassion from the compassionate and integrity from the noble, our executives more often confronted such values when stuck under a bad boss. We surmise that the dramatic example set, coupled with the inability to avoid the situation, is what made the experience so potent. And potent it was, for executives who had this kind of experience spoke in extremes: the cruelty of an "Attila the Hun" boss, feelings of disgust, humiliation, and fear. The revulsion many felt led them to vow, first, never to let themselves feel that way again and, second, never to do anything to make others feel that way either.

After considerable reflection, rising executives usually turned these how-not-to-act realizations into some guidelines for their own behavior.

Some developed matter-of-fact strategies for dealing not only with adversarial bosses but also with other nasty relationships over which they had little direct control. If the person is a roller coaster, time your moves for the upswing; if you differ in opinion on one thing, be supportive on something else; if the clash is personal, keep the interaction on a professional level, give in on the unimportant. Underlying these strategies was a tacit realization that changing the boss (or foe) was a long shot—but that changing one's self to improve the relationship was a possibility.

Others found through trial and error that, in their particular situation, none of the active strategies worked. Instead they got through the ordeal by keeping their heads down and learning a very tough lesson for aggressive, ambitious managers: patience. What they couldn't do with action, they had to do with their minds. They adapted in various ways, from convincing themselves that they worked "for the company, not the boss" to learning "to live by the boss's rules." Their patience usually paid off in the long run as they got transferred or promoted, or their bosses were fired, demoted, retired, transferred, or sometimes even promoted.

The second set of lessons from the bad bosses came as the executives figured out what a manager should do by watching another manager do it wrong. In reactions to how they were treated, or how they saw others treated, strong values emerged about how people (especially subordinates) *should* be treated and how a manager *should* act, given the responsibilities of the role. From bosses' negative acts they formed positive action guidelines for managing others.

1. *People deserve recognition for what they accomplish.* "Make those under you visible," one manager said. "Treat people in ways that respect them and their abilities," said another.

2. *People need enough rope to show what they can do, to take responsibility.* As one executive put it, "Your subordinates will always know more than you do about a given area. Let the string out as far as they can go. Ask for their input." Another told us, "People are more open when they don't feel at risk for disagreeing or asking questions."

3. *There may be more to it than meets the eye.* "Being negative often comes from insecurity," one manager discovered. "By watching the boss, I learned something about myself—when I'm not knowledgeable about something, I'm sometimes negative because I feel intimidated by those who are." Another executive seemed to suggest that an intolerable boss might not be as bad as he appeared to be. "Everyone has problems, but there are reasons. A little bit of tolerance can help you iron out the problems."

4. *You've got to accept your responsibilities.* "I worked for a guy who openly said that the best move was not to make any decisions. I learned not to be that way. You have to gather your data, then *do* something. With no decisions, there is also no feedback, no mistakes to learn from."

Lessons from Bosses: The Flawed

> I've always liked people who are eccentric, who aren't afraid to bend policies, because in the oil business, my role is to take risks.
>
> We were building a plant in Venezuela and my boss there was probably the most unusual guy I've ever met. He only came to the office when he felt like it, and he drank heavily. His real office was in a bar, and I had a hard time just finding him to go over plans.
>
> He was enormously creative, and could come up with all kinds of ways to do things. Whenever I could track him down, he would come up with radical ideas for controls or circuitry in the plant. Sitting in a bar one day, he came up with a safe way to connect a 6,000 rpm gas turbine to a 300 rpm reciprocating compressor on an offshore rig and control the natural harmonics which can make bridges, or in this case an offshore platform, fall. He just thought out a very complex solution which saved the company a lot of money, was safe, and took up less space, which is critical on a rig because there's little extra room to begin with.
>
> He taught me that you don't have to follow conventional thinking. He'd say, "Why this? How about this instead? When people tell you it can't be done, why can't it? There's a way around it." So he did two important things for me: He got me out of my channeled way of thinking (I was pretty narrow then), and he gave me a larger scope to my life. He wasn't around, so I had to make a lot of decisions on my own. His kind of teaching helped me a lot in later years.
>
> Finally, he never came to work at all and we had to let him go. He just never fit into a corporate structure.

There was a tragic air to experiences like Jim's and those of other executives who watched talented bosses do themselves in. Unlike the bosses described as purely good or bad, these "tragic" bosses possessed at the same time a remarkable talent and fatal flaws. Because of that, executives who worked for this kind of boss took away both kinds of lessons discussed earlier: learning from what the person did well and learning how to cope effectively with the flaws. But there was a new wrinkle in these experiences as many executives realized that even talented people can fail, and that failure can be their own fault. For some, the event triggered a new look at their own flaws and how those flaws might do them in.

There is no question in our minds that perceptions of good bosses neglected some flaws and of bad bosses overlooked some virtues. In that sense, then, flawed bosses like Jim's weren't all that different. If they stood out, it was because both the strengths and the weaknesses were extreme, creating a highly visible paradox that negated simplistic judgments. Perhaps the unspoken lessons had to do with managerial dilemmas: Just how long should a flaw be overlooked because of a real strength? Our study of derailed executives clearly showed that exactly this dynamic—strengths blinding others to weaknesses—played a central part in selecting executives who failed to reach their potential.

Implications for Organizations

Coaching and mentoring programs abound as organizations attempt to have more senior people pass along their knowledge, usually in skill areas. This strategy takes advantage of only one of the many possible ways that special bosses might teach. From what successful executives told us, we would suggest the following modifications.

In considering a new assignment for a developing executive, one should take a careful look at the boss (and the higher level managers) who goes with it. Since bosses change jobs too, a new boss may be a "new assignment" for the subordinate as well. Depending on what a person needs to learn, exposure to a different kind of boss may be a more important consideration than the assignment per se. Whether or not the boss is a "good teacher" may not be all that important—it appears more critical that the developing executive is able to learn from other people's strengths and weaknesses.

We are not suggesting that high-potential managers should be deliberately assigned to ogres. Not only is this cruel, but keeping such people in managerial roles conveys far more destructive values to the organization than any offsetting individual gain could justify. Yet frequent changing of bosses won't cut it either—we seldom heard stories of learning from mediocre bosses. When we talk of variety in bosses, we really mean variety in the exceptional qualities those bosses possess.

The reason is not simply that an executive might learn new skills from such variety, or even an overoptimistic view of vicarious learning. Rather, working for someone is a direct experience with value-laden outcomes. "I learned the value of rope because I was given rope; the value of innovation because it solved a problem I had; the value of inspiration because I was inspired." They felt the impact of how they were treated and how they reacted to it; they didn't have to guess how others felt or rely on feedback to figure it out. So although in one sense the learning from bosses was vicarious, in the more important values sense the learning was a direct jolt.

Variety was a good bet, then, because learning from bosses is at once idiosyncratic and potent. In addition to the possible learning we have already discussed, exposure to a variety of bosses can reduce the probability of derailment later in the career for at least four reasons.

First, the kinds of things learned from other people can balance what's learned from assignments. Successful completion of demanding assignments, as discussed earlier, is the breeding ground for self-confidence, toughness, and independence. Exposure to bosses is a primary source of several balancing attributes—human values to temper the toughness, respect for others and for the responsibilities of a manager to blunt the potential arrogance of confidence, and understanding how to direct and motivate others as a complement to the independence (and power) of the managerial role.

Second, exposure to a variety of exceptional bosses can provide learning that more often comes from assignments but can come from other people. As we noted earlier, gaps *can* be filled in by the right person at the right time.

Third, variety in bosses can offset some of the reasons executives derail. Managers who have worked effectively with many different kinds of bosses have demonstrated their ability to adapt to superiors with very different styles. Those who have survived rounds with bad bosses have proven their composure under stress and, presumably, their ability to focus on the business problems that need solving rather than on the boss's personality.

Finally, some executives we studied derailed because of their perceived overdependence on a mentor or advocate. Staying with the same boss too long or being too closely identified with a single mentor led some senior executives to doubt the manager's ability to act independently of the boss, to wonder if he were a clone.

What Bosses Can Teach

In summary, we have seen in this chapter that developing executives report learning a wide variety of specific skills from various exceptional bosses. As we have noted, however, the values lessons associated with watching a significant boss's actions take on meaning larger than the specifics. In fact, four lessons from bosses were reported more frequently than specific skills, and in them lies the heart of the experience:

- **Management Values.** Future executives learned proper and improper deportment for a manager and how abstractions like trust, integrity, and ethics play out in day-to-day events with other people.
- **Human Values.** The difference between how people should be treated as people and how they were treated was driven in by similar events.
- **What Executives Are Like.** The good, the bad, and the flawed taught future executives that a variety of people can succeed, and that there was no one best style of behavior.
- **Politics.** "How things really work around here," who gets rewarded and punished for what, how to push through a decision were demonstrated by an assortment of admirable and not-so-admirable characters.

As with any experience, the place to focus is not on the experience itself but on what the manager takes away from it (see

Individual Lessons

Setting and Implementing Agendas
- Technical/professional skills
- All about the business one is in
- Strategic thinking
- Shouldering full responsibility
- Building and using structure and control systems
- Innovative problem-solving methods

Handling Relationships
- **HANDLING POLITICAL SITUATIONS**
- Getting people to implement solutions
- **WHAT EXECUTIVES ARE LIKE**
- How to work with executives
- Strategies of negotiation
- Dealing with people over whom you have no authority
- Understanding other people's perspectives
- Dealing with conflict
- Directing and motivating subordinates
- Developing other people
- Confronting subordinate performance problems
- Managing former bosses and peers

Basic Values
- You can't manage everything all alone
- **SENSITIVITY TO THE HUMAN SIDE OF MANAGEMENT**
- **BASIC MANAGEMENT VALUES**

Executive Temperament
- Being tough when necessary
- Self-confidence
- Coping with situations beyond your control
- Persevering through adversity
- Coping with ambiguous situations
- Use (and abuse) of power

Personal Awareness
- The balance between work and personal life
- Knowing what really excites you about work
- Personal limits and blind spots

> - Taking charge of your career
> - Recognizing and seizing opportunities
>
> *Major Learning Thrusts*
>
> - The importance of values-in-action to managerial effectiveness
> - How people should be treated in an organization and the manager's special responsibility to subordinates
> - The potentially damaging effect of hidden flaws and of strengths that can become weaknesses
>
> See Lindsey, et al., *Key Events in Executives' Lives,* Technical Report No. 32 (Greensboro, N.C.: Center for Creative Leadership, 1987), 149–171.

Figure 3–1. *The Potential Lessons of Other People*

figure 3–1). In the case of bosses, any skill learned may not show up until later (as with Gene and Jim), when it must be applied in a new situation. More evident (even if more nebulous) are the values lessons etched by the experience. From the bad, one hopes to learn not to be that way. From the good, one hopes to learn not only personal lessons but also things that can be passed on by their own behavior toward subordinates in the future.

Rising executives are bosses too, and, intentionally or not, are constantly making value statements about themselves. Our research and that of others suggests that most managers are unaware of how closely they are watched and are unaware of the symbolic impact of their actions.[7] In our study, when executives reported something they did to subordinates, they believed it was well received 80 percent of the time, but when they mentioned something their bosses did to them, their reaction was often negative.[8] Managers, like the rest of us, tend to attribute good actions to self and blame bad actions on others.

Feedback to rising executives on how they are perceived is critical—as teachers of skills, as models of behavior, as coaches, and as representatives of the political system. Stories will be told about them. They too will teach.

4
Hardships

We believe that any developmental event creates a tension between where a person is and where the person wants to be. This tension triggers some sort of adaptive response. Because of this, nearly all developmental events involve a confrontation with adverse circumstances—intractable people or troublesome business problems—obstacles that must be overcome.

Challenging assignments, as we have seen, are filled with these tensions. A fix-it carries with it the challenge of coping with problem subordinates; starting from scratch forces one to confront the limits of endurance; in line-to-staff switches, one is faced with ambiguity; project/task force assignments often involve a sense of loss of control; and leaps in scope present the troublesome situation of having to manage former peers or even former bosses. Yet, though adversity was a part of all assignments and played a role in learning, adversity was not the focus. The focus of assignments was on the lessons of success.

Such lessons are largely external ones: how to solve problems to cope with *job demands,* handle a potpourri of *other people,* or learn skills quickly to accomplish a *task.* Successfully completed assignments test one's resilience and wit in dealing with tough external circumstances, but they don't test how one comes back from utter failure. On the other hand, a failed assignment emphasizes lessons different from those of a challenge successfully met. When faced with their own failure, executives who learned from it did not reflect only on externalities. Instead, they turned inward and took a hard look at themselves.

As we saw in the last chapter, working for a difficult boss was certainly a hardship of kinds, but the lessons drawn from such an experience were different from those we will discuss in this chapter. Watching the unscrupulous action of a "bad" boss led to some vicarious learning about how *not* to act, but the impact was different from that of pure hardships. The difference lies in the fact that the reprehensible actions were someone else's, not the manager's own. Watching the failures of others often provokes a reflection on one's values, an examination of how one might or might not act in a similar situation, but rarely do such vicarious lessons provoke a direct confrontation with self.

A sense of failure and aloneness distinguish the hardships of this chapter from the other developmental events. Something the executives did or failed to do caused things to go wrong. Even when they were victims of circumstance—when they were wrongly accused or when a worker was killed in an accident—these executives turned inward. Was there something they hadn't done or something they simply couldn't handle? Had a fatal flaw, hidden all these years, been revealed?

The hardships of this chapter arose out of five types of events. We will discuss each type of event separately, focusing first on the principal challenges of each and then on the lessons drawn by the executives we studied. These five types of hardship events were:

1. A *personal trauma* threatening the health and well-being of the executive or the executive's family.

2. A *career setback* involving demotions and missed promotions.

3. *Changing jobs,* in which some executives risked their careers to get out of a dead-end job.

4. *Business mistakes,* in which bad judgment and poor decisions led to failure.

5. A *subordinate performance problem* forcing the executive to confront people with issues of incompetence or with problems such as alcoholism.

These hardships can provoke several types of lessons involving a confrontation with self. The executives learned lessons about themselves in relationship to others, their career aspirations, their capacity to overcome defeat and fear, and their ability to adapt in a sometimes arbitrary world. In each confrontation they came up short. Therein lay the lesson. As research has shown, the recognition and acceptance of limitations, followed by an effort to redirect oneself, are characteristic of successful people in general.[1] It was how the executives responded, then, not the event itself, that is the key to understanding the value of these hardships.

Personal Trauma

Trauma is life at its extreme. The stories of personal trauma were often told to us in neutral words, as if a vivid description of the emotional impact would open the door to feelings that some of the executives sought to keep locked up. Executives mentioned various kinds of crisis experiences: personal illness or injury, divorce and family breakups, military combat duty, and work-related accidents and fatalities. Except for the military situations and some of the accidents, the executives played more than a small part in these nightmares. They caused or contributed to them. Once the event occurred and the initial shock wore off, they all faced the same out-of-control feelings. Their expectations for themselves had been dashed; they were forced to question their accustomed behavior; many began to wonder if they'd brought on their troubles by their selfishness and ambition. Had they run too fast after a career and not paid enough attention to others? Had their lives become unbalanced enough to topple over?

Many of the personal traumas centered on crises at home that may have been precipitated by a growing imbalance in the value an executive put on work. Most of the executives had focused on their careers during their twenties and thirties, possibly because as goal-oriented, achievement-driven people by nature, they found in the workplace the variety, challenge, and excitement that hooked them. Successes reinforced the need for more success, and they became more career-oriented and less family-oriented. On a daily basis, family and personal life couldn't compete with the excitement of work.

Whether their lives became precariously out of balance depended, of course, on individual situations. Some executives found a way to stay close to their families. Some had accommodating families who accepted the fact that their personal lives clearly came second. Others were lucky and were spared a traumatic reminder. A common tactic for the executives was to try to keep their personal and work lives separate, a curious strategy which usually meant that work could intrude on personal life, but not the other way around. For some it was probably a genuine attempt to buffer one sphere from the other, but for others it served to shut off some unpleasant truths. One's image as a family man or a nice guy might be tarnished. Some changes might have to be made, and something might have to be given up.

One executive we interviewed told us the story of his marriage, which he had grown to believe was nearly ideal. Others thought of him and his wife as the "golden couple." But in his almost total focus on work, he had grown blind to the emerging problems. Not until his wife became so depressed over their relationship that she was unable to get out of bed in the morning did he begin to see the problem. Others told similar stories that centered on the effects of emotional problems in their children—poor grades in school, delinquency, drugs.

Of all the developmental events, hardships (and traumas in particular) guard their lessons best. The temptation to distance oneself from the event can be compelling. There is always someone or something else one can blame. Disclaiming responsibility for the event can set up a chain reaction in which one also denies the response to it. A trauma can be used to justify cynicism or fatalism or withdrawal or overcompensation. The choice between relying on one's less mature defenses or looking inward to find lessons is one in which immaturity often wins out because it provides pat explanations. It is easy to tell oneself that a rational person in an irrational world had better be on guard but need not really change. After all, the irrational and arbitrary world is the problem. This sort of response to a traumatic event will hardly lead to learning.

The first step in learning from a trauma, or any hardship event, is arguably the hardest: absorbing the suffering rather than reacting against it. One of the executives we interviewed told an unusual story; yet, even with its oddity, its implications for learning from hardships are clear. He had given a subordinate a particularly bad performance rating, a "slap in the face" intended to jolt the man out of his counterproductive attitudes. The response was stunning, to say the least, and didn't come from the subordinate. It came from his wife, who showed up the next day waving a pistol, threatening to kill the executive. She was arrested but was soon released on bail. The executive had to be guarded day and night and had to send his family away. The executive's immediate response was naturally to lay blame for the incident elsewhere. The wife was emotionally unstable; he had only been doing his job; it was his responsibility to correct poor performance. Sending his family away deepened his resentment toward the subordinate's wife but also gave him time to reflect. He eventually came to realize that this incident might have reflected in general on his relationships with others.

Three things stood out as he thought about his relationships: conversations with his co-workers were predominantly task-based; he did not have warm relationships at work; some of his best subordinates were at times irritated by his sharply critical style. This was when the impact sank in—not that he deserved what happened, but that there was meaning in the experience. He typically showed little need or sensitivity for others, and in various ways they returned the insult. There was more to it, though. Saying he displayed little need for others was just another way of saying he tried to do it all himself. The result of that overintensity could be an angry spouse or personal relationships that were tenuous. He supposed he had been more of a task-based manager than a person, and, in his quest to do it all, he had come up against one of his limits.

This is an extreme tale, but events at the extremes were often the goad that had forced the managers we interviewed to look inward. In general we found that four learning themes emerged from this kind of insight.

Recognition of Personal Limits. Like the busy manager who, after a fatal plant accident, finally called in help for a safety program, or the manager threatened by a subordinate's wife, some managers saw their traumatic experiences as symbols of a blind spot, a flaw in their character. They had tried to do it all and had hurt people in their haste. The experiences served as powerful reminders that they, too, were limited and subject to human frailty.

Sensitivity to Others. Some managers saw a need for a more humane approach to managing people. After a devastating divorce and a successful remarriage, one manager discovered that the energy he put into his second marriage spilled over into work: "I learned that driving concern and overintensity make a less effective manager. Now I'm reasonable—I learn how fast a person can go and I push him to that point only." Another lesson on how to motivate subordinates he learned from being badly injured: "I was a football player at age sixteen, and I broke my neck. I was told I'd never play again. Being an athlete had created for me my whole sense of purpose. The doctor spent a lot of time helping me with the psychological implications, showing me that I had to find another way to excel. Now, as a manager, I help others find goals appropriate for them."

Coping with Events beyond Your Own Control. Especially as a result of combat and acts of nature, managers talked about the need to control their reactions when they couldn't control the situation. Hanging in and persevering through the event were common refrains. "When things get tough . . . don't second-guess past decisions. Keep going in the same direction unless you have evidence that another is better," one said. Another remarked: "Learn to play mental tricks on yourself to keep yourself sane. Think: 'Nothing anybody can do to me can be worse than this.' Use this to pump yourself up to get through tough situations."

The Balance between Life and Work. The most common lesson from traumas was a reminder to managers that their lives were out of whack. Many rummaged through their achievements and realized that while achievements brought satisfaction, only relationships brought joy. Their traumas caused them to reevaluate what was important to them. One manager left the company to help his son work through some problems; another refused an important transfer and eventually resigned so that his retarded daughter's development wouldn't be disrupted by having to move away from the therapy center. The manager who was threatened by the angry wife realized that he could be sensitive to people without sacrificing his effectiveness as a manager. In fact, he and others found they could increase their effectiveness by allowing the complementary lessons of their personal lives to seep more into their work.

In a sense, all the lessons from traumas helped managers regain a sense of balance. Whether it was in how they reacted to fate or how they sought to reintegrate their view of themselves as a person and as a manager, balance was the issue. They sought to regain control of their reactions and of situations and to influence how others viewed them.

Traumas may shock people into changing for the better, or they may shock them into collapse. Mercifully, the latter possibility was rarely cited. The more general question here is, are more successful executives better able to achieve the balances we have mentioned throughout this book? Are they more likely to be tough and sensitive, be confident yet know their limits, persevere through nightmarish events, and put a lot of energy into both their personal and work lives?

The answer, in a general sense, is yes. One of the reasons for executive success is this capacity to adapt—to endure the toughest of situations and make a major change as a result.[2] In a specific sense, however, the answer is maybe. Many of the executives we interviewed exhibited no awareness of the need for balance, speaking of toughness and sensitivity, for example, as if they were unrelated. A few candidly stated that their families came second: "For most of my career it's been 80 percent career and 20 percent family. I probably wouldn't do it differently."

Another said, "I don't get equal joy from the kids and working around the house. My wife and I are having a lot of tension over my career."

For many executives it seemed that only hardships, especially a wrenching trauma, could force them to ask whether their professional and personal lives were as they should be, or if they could really cope with tough situations. Only the shovel-in-the-face kinds of events created a need for deep self-examination, and even then there were no guarantees. The lessons taken away might be cynical or fatalistic, and even helpful lessons might soon be forgotten in the crush of a new job assignment. Balance is not a state but a tension, and even a trauma endured and learned from does not preclude one's life from tipping over again. (See figure 4–1 for a summary of the lessons of personal trauma.)

Individual Lessons

Setting and Implementing Agendas
- Technical/professional skills
- All about the business one is in
- Strategic thinking
- Shouldering full responsibility
- Building and using structure and control systems
- Innovative problem-solving methods

Handling Relationships
- Handling political situations
- Getting people to implement solutions
- What executives are like
- How to work with executives
- Strategies of negotiation
- Dealing with people over whom you have no authority
- Understanding other people's perspectives
- Dealing with conflict
- Directing and motivating subordinates
- Developing other people
- Confronting subordinate performance problems
- Managing former bosses and peers

Basic Values
- You can't manage everything all alone
- SENSITIVITY TO THE HUMAN SIDE OF MANAGEMENT
- Basic management values

Executive Temperament
- Being tough when necessary
- Self-confidence
- COPING WITH SITUATIONS BEYOND YOUR CONTROL
- PERSEVERING THROUGH ADVERSITY
- Coping with ambiguous situations
- USE (AND ABUSE) OF POWER

Personal Awareness
- THE BALANCE BETWEEN WORK AND PERSONAL LIFE
- Knowing what really excites you about work
- PERSONAL LIMITS AND BLIND SPOTS
- Taking charge of your career
- Recognizing and seizing opportunities

Major Learning Thrusts

Sensitivity to Others

Like the manager who gave the "rough" performance appraisal, many learned some lessons of compassion as a result of pain.

Coping with Events beyond One's Control

No one can control events, but we can control how we respond—facing the situation and persevering through it were common refrains.

Recognition of Personal Limits/The Balance between Work and Personal life

Being brought up short was the central theme of personal traumas, and reflecting on one's inadequacies and blind spots often led to a decision to reconsider how one lives one's life.

See Esther Lindsey, et al., *Key Events in Executives' Lives,* Technical Report No. 32 (Greensboro, N.C.: Center for Creative Leadership, 1987), 137–146.

Figure 4–1. *The Potential Lessons of Personal Traumas*

Career Setbacks

Even though the executives we interviewed were considered to be highly successful, about 15 percent of them told us that they had missed expected promotions or had been transferred to undesirable jobs or had been demoted. Some had even been fired. Although the circumstances of these setbacks varied, the executives reported learning lessons about themselves, about their organizations and corporate politics, or about jobs.

Learning about Self

One executive we interviewed had once overplayed his hand: "Having achieved almost arrogant self-confidence," he told us, "and because of my strong dedication to my division and to the development of my subordinates, I got into a serious conflict with the head of personnel over total control of my employees. I was transferred." Another was fired "for not being entrepreneurial." Another was asked to leave "when I ran out of people who would work with me."

When these managers were fired or demoted or "transferred" because of their mistakes, they were forced to confront the truth about themselves. They were forced to recognize that they had flaws and that these flaws made a difference. They couldn't keep getting by, much less continue advancing, unless they found some way to reduce their deficiencies. But facing and correcting deficiencies was not the end of their confrontation with self.

Many of the executives we interviewed, particularly those who had suffered a setback prior to age thirty-five, talked about the need to examine their expectations for themselves in a more realistic light. One executive, who had resigned in anger from a large CPA firm when he was thirty, told us, "I was a fast-track manager, having been promoted in record time to each new management position. All of the partners on my key assignments had recommended me for promotion. Nevertheless, the management committee decided that I needed more seasoning and did not accept the promotion recommendation that year."

After he resigned, and after the anger wore off, he realized the management committee had been right after all. "Performance is not the only criterion for promotion," he told us. "Maturity, seasoning, and knowing the right people are also key elements for promotion to senior management positions. Early in one's career, you tend to set absolute targets: 'I must be promoted by a certain time; if not, I'm a failure.' I sure could have used some career counseling to overcome my unrealistic expectations as a young manager."

Unrealistic expectations could also cause young managers to misperceive the intent of a job assignment. Many believed that only a promotion was worthwhile. Any other assignment was a demotion or a "lousy job." Yet, as we have seen in the chapter on assignments, many developmental jobs do not involve a promotion. Functional transfers, time-limited projects, and important task force assignments are frequently given to young managers to help them develop skills and gain the necessary seasoning to cope with senior management positions. Some of the executives remembered feeling that their careers had reached a dead-end when they were reassigned without being promoted, only to realize later that the assignment had been given to them as a developmental opportunity in recognition of their potential. Perhaps their organization could have made the intent clearer, but a naive understanding of how managers develop was also responsible for their initial negative reaction.

Learning about Organizations and Politics

Not all of the executives in our study faced setbacks because of skill deficiencies or unreasonable expectations. Some simply lost out in a merger, or earned enmity from a boss, or were double-crossed, or were passed over for promotion in favor of a more politically acceptable candidate.

Most of these kinds of setbacks triggered cynical reactions ("Never trust the corporation"; "Flash and resumes win promotions"; "You've got to cover your ass"), but none so much as mergers and reorganizations.

Almost half of the executives mentioned a merger or reorganization in response to the question, "When were you worn out or fed up?" During these organizational upheavals, arbitrary formulas for determining who filled management roles (for example, 70 percent from company A and 30 percent from company B), the consolidation of functions (which often meant there was a loser for each remaining management position), and the clash of intermingling cultures caused a great deal of stress. Talented managers ended up in staff roles or in jobs with little visibility or clout. They felt these jobs were beneath them, involving skills they'd already mastered and challenges they'd already faced. Overwhelmingly, the lessons of these times revolved around how to persist in an unfair world. Few saw their situation as one within their control, and so focused their efforts on coping with it rather than tilting at windmills. This coping involved adopting attitudes that preserved their sense of equilibrium.

Some managers took the attitude that everything doesn't rise and fall with the present. Some waited to be rescued and were. Others had faith that top management had a pervasive view and they would ascend once again.

Some vowed to be single-minded, figuring they were in the job they were in and they might as well succeed at it. They absorbed the disappointment, dug in, and tried to find some worthwhile goals to accomplish. Most banked on self-reliance, finding a sense of purpose in what they could accomplish as well as their ability to withstand the punishment of an ill-fitting job.

Overlaying these personal reactions were some that involved the organization. The executives in our study typically responded in one of two ways. Some saw the situation in a mostly political light and determined to stay visible, keep others informed, and continue to sell themselves while disassociating themselves from those of questionable competence or integrity. A more cynical political response involved seeing it as a game to play, a distasteful pandering, all good impressions and fluff.

The second type of response was to create emotional distance. "I stopped caring about my job on an emotional level," one executive told us. A less extreme kind of distancing was to focus on the job as a profession, or on subordinates as friends and colleagues and try to ignore the larger organizational picture.

In general, however, the reactions of the managers we interviewed to being "done in" were rarely totally cynical. Most seemed to recognize that unfair situations were a part of life and that coping with them was a test of their fortitude and resilience.

But this type of event was a rude awakening. For people whose sense of worth was tied to their excellence as managers of people and resources, the capriciousness of the event was brutal. To be reassigned to less important jobs without regard for their skill disillusioned most and made many of them angry. Even though many of their lessons had the normal here's-how-to-get-through-this-one flavor, this event showed executives at their most caustic and least forgiving. "Even the eventual chairman was demoted during the merger"; "I was painted with the same brush as managers who were fired"; and "People will burn you to save themselves" were typical of the angry remarks we heard.

Regardless of the intensity of these reactions, however, we heard nothing about managers resorting to grandstand tactics. We heard of no one who made a scene or tried to elicit sympathy. Instead, they waited and did their jobs. Some avoided cynicism, some grew scars overnight, and some never realized the scars were growing.

Learning about Jobs

Sometimes a career setback involved neither a demotion nor a reorganization. Sometimes the setback happened because a job became meaningless for the manager in it. He'd been in it too long, or outgrown it, or been placed in a job he'd already mastered. The job was demeaning, trivial, the kind of position appropriate for those with less drive. Occasionally the job was at the other extreme and was too tough.

From these jobs, managers found out what they didn't like: low responsibility, low stress, low visibility jobs; or conversely, disorganized, chaotic operations with no plan, no objectives, no recognition for outstanding performance, political quagmires in which everything turned on personality, or jobs that involved bosses who were thorns even on their best days.

But if they learned what they didn't like, they also learned what they wanted: "I like to run businesses, not hustle business"; "I like risk"; "I like unstructured, short-term challenges." From these realizations, it was only a short distance to the next question: "How do I get there from here?"

Waiting for rescue was an option, as was working hard at a job they didn't like. But these possibilities were usually dismissed in favor of taking personal charge of their careers. Although they couldn't guarantee themselves the career they wanted, they could be prepared when opportunities arose, and they could perhaps create some opportunities for themselves. (Figure 4–2 summarizes the lessons of career setbacks.)

Individual Lessons

Setting and Implementing Agendas
- Technical/professional skills
- All about the business one is in
- Strategic thinking
- Shouldering full responsibility
- Building and using structure and control systems
- Innovative problem-solving methods

Handling Relationships
- **HANDLING POLITICAL SITUATIONS**
- Getting people to implement solutions
- What executives are like
- How to work with executives
- Strategies of negotiation
- Dealing with people over whom you have no authority
- Understanding other people's perspectives
- Dealing with conflict
- Directing and motivating subordinates
- Developing other people
- Confronting subordinate performance problems
- Managing former bosses and peers

Basic Values
- You can't manage everything all alone
- Sensitivity to the human side of management
- Basic management values

Executive Temperament
- Being tough when necessary
- Self-confidence
- **COPING WITH SITUATIONS BEYOND YOUR CONTROL**
- **PERSEVERING THROUGH ADVERSITY**
- Coping with ambiguous situations
- Use (and abuse) of power

Personal Awareness
- The balance between work and personal life
- Knowing what really excites you about work
- **PERSONAL LIMITS AND BLIND SPOTS**
- **TAKING CHARGE OF YOUR CAREER**
- Recognizing and seizing opportunities

Major Learning Thrusts

Self

Managers learned to face their limitations and scale down unrealistic expectations.

Organizations

Managers learned how to cope with the vagaries of losing out due to organizational politics, mergers, and the like. Their lessons ran from pragmatic to cynical around whom to sell their ideas to, and how, and the need for patience and a long-term view of their situations.

Jobs

Managers learned what sorts of jobs they didn't like and, from this, what they did.

See Esther Lindsey, et al., *Key Events in Executives' Lives,* Technical Report No. 32 (Greensboro, N.C.: Center for Creative Leadership, 1987), 105–116.

Figure 4–2. *The Potential Lessons of a Career Setback*

Changing Jobs

What happened next was up to the individual manager. Most of those we interviewed endured the tough times and eventually got back on track. But for some, the issue was not that the job was unbearable or had a stigma attached to it; instead, the problem was that the job had become too comfortable for them. They had mastered it, or the technical field they were in had lost its allure. In short, they were bored and discontented. They wanted out. "I had an R&D job, six assignments in five years," one future executive told us. "My supervisor left, and I expected the phone to ring for ten days. I didn't get the job, and I couldn't believe it. I went to the head of R&D, and he told me I was great but I needed seven to eight years' more seasoning. He told me I could only work in R&D because, after all, I was a chemical engineer, and there were no other openings. I didn't believe him. I went and *reapplied* to [the same company] and was interviewed by someone I knew. I got to pick my own job in operations."

Changing jobs or careers has its own risks. Breaking a career rut is not as straightforward as going from a bad job to a good job. The managers we interviewed realized that if you want to do something exciting, you have to leave the safe behind. The trade they made involved losing first; any gain was uncertain and would come much later.

Most of those we talked to who broke out of a rut traded in successful careers for an uncertain future. They left corporations they'd been with for a decade, arranged for a staff-to-line switch to get where the action was, went from the line to corporate staff to broaden their business perspective, took lateral and downward shifts to get into new areas, or issued stark challenges to higher management: "I requested a transfer from marketing research to product management, for which I had no previous experience or training. My action words were: 'If I can't do the job successfully in six months, fire me.'"

Managers forced these changes out of discontent, sometimes from desperation. Whether they seized opportunities that floated by or created their own, the common denominator in seeking these changes was to go for something that could excite them again. They took a chance in trying their hand at operations, or corporate strategy, or marketing, or in an overseas assignment because the challenge got their juices flowing again. "If you see an opportunity that is a challenge . . . have the courage to give it a try," one said. Another saw comfort as the enemy of career growth: "When you get comfortable, look for something else."

What the managers we interviewed saw as breaking a career rut is the flip side of the demotions, missed promotions, and bad jobs they described. From setbacks, they learned how organizations could derail them, or how they could derail themselves. In breaking out of a rut, they learned how to save themselves from present or future career stagnation. Both experiences involved loss and the fear or the reality of failure. And both experiences offered the same discomfiting advice: It's up to you to take charge of your career. You can stay or leave, but either way offers little control over events. Unlike assignments, where the challenge lay in overcoming obstacles to achieve success, here the challenges were visceral. Could you rise from the ashes? Did you know enough about yourself to know what you wanted? And most important, did you have the guts to stay when that seemed best, and when it didn't, to change?

The executives we interviewed who had faced such a choice were divided on the issue of career planning. About two-thirds thought you could plan ahead *in general*. The rest advised concentrating on the job at hand. In our study of their development, we saw little, if any, evidence of systematic career planning in the sense of setting developmental goals and selecting jobs to achieve the goals. If anything, the career moves of these executives were more random than programmed. In facing the critical choice of whether to stay or leave, therefore, these executives did not try to predict which would be better. Instead, they used a few down-to-earth decision rules:

Stick to the Business Core. If they were in a core line area or had good credentials for line jobs, they usually stayed. If they were in a peripheral unit, they found a way to get to a core job somewhere else.

Match the Business to Your Personal Style. If they were entrepreneurially oriented, they sought entrepreneurial jobs. If they craved action, they stayed in fast-paced organizations or got out of slow ones.

Timing Is Critical. Except for a few who bounced around early in their careers trying to find an occupation that interested them, these executives were not job hoppers. They had commonly been with a company or even in a given job seven to thirteen years before they forced a change. Even in the darkest of situations, most of them hung on for two years or more. Partly, they found in the job a personal challenge: Could they make something of this job? Did they have the patience and perseverance to see it through? And partly, their reasoning was instrumental. There are many ways to be branded in an organization, and one of the most damning is "Can't stand the heat" or "Folds under pressure." Reacting angrily to a bad job can easily get one branded as petulant or volatile. Most executives waited the situation out for a while, testing themselves and testing their organization. Thus, when they did break away, their moves were hardly precipitous.

Serendipity Is the Best Placement Service. The vast majority of job switches we heard about appeared to be self-directed and opportunistic, not the result of resume "floating" or brokering through corporate headhunters. Managers knew what they wanted after *years* of soul searching, and they sometimes grabbed an opportunity that excited them. Some called this luck, but it was really a case of preparation meeting opportunity. One executive told of his greatest career move coming from a chance lunch meeting. But he was prepared, he knew what he wanted, and, at some level, he was already looking for a more challenging opportunity.

Behind all of this was an overriding philosophy that career moves are best determined by emotional contrast, not in some formula of the right job or the right career path. A career crisis did not lead them to a dispassionate analysis but to a visceral response involving feelings about perseverance, about coping in a tough world, and about personal responsibility for career. Since the future was unknowable and organizations somewhat whimsical, the executives we studied went with the one predictor they could count on. When all the data were in, they decided on the basis of what *felt* like the right thing to do. (Figure 4–3 summarizes the lessons of changing jobs.)

Individual Lessons

Setting and Implementing Agendas
- Technical/professional skills
- All about the business one is in
- Strategic thinking
- Shouldering full responsibility
- Building and using structure and control systems
- Innovative problem-solving methods

Handling Relationships
- Handling political situations
- Getting people to implement solutions
- What executives are like
- How to work with executives
- Strategies of negotiation
- Dealing with people over whom you have no authority
- Understanding other people's perspectives
- Dealing with conflict
- Directing and motivating subordinates
- Developing other people
- Confronting subordinate performance problems
- Managing former bosses and peers

Basic Values
- You can't manage everything all alone
- Sensitivity to the human side of management
- Basic management values

(Continued)

Figure 4–3. *The Potential Lessons of Changing Jobs*

> *Executive Temperament*
> - Being tough when necessary
> - Self-confidence
> - Coping with situations beyond your control
> - Persevering through adversity
> - Coping with ambiguous situations
> - Use (and abuse) of power
>
> *Personal Awareness*
> - The balance between work and personal life
> - **KNOWING WHAT REALLY EXCITES YOU ABOUT WORK**
> - Personal limits and blind spots
> - **TAKING CHARGE OF YOUR CAREER**
> - **RECOGNIZING AND SEIZING OPPORTUNITIES**
>
> *Major Learning Thrust*
>
> *Taking Charge of Your Career*
>
> > Managers decided what they wanted to do and why they wanted to do it, then did it. They learned to rely on themselves in seeking opportunities that would unblock their careers.
>
> See Esther Lindsey, et al., *Key Events in Executives' Lives,* Technical Report No. 32 (Greensboro, N.C.: Center for Creative Leadership, 1987), 117–126.

Figure 4–3. (*Continued*)

Business Mistakes

Most of the executives we interviewed confessed to having made a least one (sometimes several) serious business mistakes in their careers. These included costly ideas that didn't work out, deals that fell through, failures to take advantage of opportunities, and conflicts that got out of hand. We might have expected that these mistakes were mostly due to a lack of knowledge or to bad business judgment, but according to the executives we interviewed, this was not so. Instead, the leading cause of business mistakes was some kind of a failure to deal properly with other people. Specifically, the mistake usually stemmed from a misjudgment of the importance of other people to the success of an idea or project and involved such things as failing to get or give adequate information, neglecting to obtain necessary support, and failing to forge agreements in advance.

These mishandled relationships leading to business mistakes fell broadly into three classes: relationships with superiors, with subordinates, and with peers and outsiders.

Where superiors were concerned, the principal way in which the relationships were mishandled involved "surprising the boss." One manager, for example, developed an elaborate strategic plan to help divisions of the company invest in R&D, but didn't mention it to anyone above him. When he presented it to a division executive, "The guy tore it up in front of me and threw it in the waste can."

Where subordinates were concerned, the major problems developed when a manager underestimated the importance of his or her subordinates. This was often manifested when a manager would expect subordinates to achieve results without first gaining their commitment to accomplishing the results. Sometimes the manager's attitude was accompanied by displays of arrogance and intolerance. "I was intolerant of incompetence," one executive remembered. "I was impetuous, and if I didn't think someone was as good as he should have been, I treated him harshly. It was a big surprise to me when my plans failed."

Where peers and outsiders were concerned, business mistakes revolved around the failure to get adequate information, support, or agreement from peer managers in other departments or from clients, partners, or contractors. In addition, some managers reported that they had not taken enough care to understand the philosophy and values of the peers or outsiders they were dealing with, and that this often added to the problem.

For the executives we interviewed, the learning from a business mistake depended on the nature of the mistake. When they were caught in a capricious situation—as when a currency devaluation or a franchisee sellout or a shutdown ordered from above wrecked their plans—their lessons had an I-felt-like-I'd-spent-a-day-on-the-wrong-end-of-a-firing-range flavor. They spoke of tenacity in the face of impossible situations, discussed strategic countermoves, and sometimes made cynical remarks about upper management. They seemed to view being caught in a disastrous business situation they could do little about as just another type of adversity to endure. Their lessons dealt with how they coped, not their own shortcomings.

When they smelled a political scam, they were as scathing as ever. One manager exceeded his authority in making a purchase and was threatened with dismissal by several levels of superiors. Irate, he got them together and chewed them out, but the denouement to the event made him even angrier. His improper purchase "resulted in a several-million-dollar profit after taxes and three layers of management took credit for it. For my efforts, I got only a rating of average on my next performance appraisal."

So, externally caused (or perceived) failures created lessons that were cynical or involved learning to endure, or both, depending on the circumstances. In contrast, mistakes that managers saw themselves as being responsible for triggered an opposite response—intensely internal, harshly self-critical. Although it is tempting to say that some people have the courage to learn from their mistakes while some blame them on others, there seem to be three general conditions that set the stage for learning from one's mistakes:

The Event Must Be Very, Very, Specific. When a cause-and-effect relationship was unclear, managers couldn't seem to sort out what to feel responsible about. Could they have anticipated a currency devaluation or a franchisee selling out to a competitor? Would it have mattered if they had? When managers could not know if their actions would have mattered, their lessons were often abstract, strategic ruminations about how to avoid the situation in general. But when the cause-and-effect relationship was clear ("I blew it with so and so because . . ."), the chance was much greater that they would see the consequences and also accept responsibility for their piece of the problem.

The Cards Must Be on the Table. For a variety of reasons, including matters of confidence and simply not thinking to do it, executives sometimes don't give younger managers the straight scoop on why a particular decision was made. But for obvious reasons, younger managers need to know why things affecting them happen. When managers are ignorant of why things happened as they did, they tend to explain consequences in terms of personalities and politics. When they have information about what is happening and why, they're in a much better position to assess their own contribution to the mess.

The Organization's Position on Mistakes Must Be Delineated. All organizations have elaborate reward systems, but few have anything approximating mistake systems. Mistakes are handled by exception and, except for illegal activities or exceedingly costly mistakes, are left up to individual bosses to adjudicate. Over a period of time, the aggregated actions of these individual bosses add up to the cultural reality of how an organization deals with mistakes. By watching bosses in these situations, and by hearing organizational "war stories," younger managers learn the answer to the endemic questions: "What happens around here if you make a big mistake? Will it be fatal?"

Most companies pay homage to "thoughtful mistakes" or "stretch mistakes." Such corporate attitudes are healthy, not because "everyone makes mistakes" but because people managing human systems in an unpredictable, loosely connected world are particularly prone to make them. If managers couldn't learn from their mistakes, there would be no one left to manage anything more testy than the company picnic.

But companies that may excel in fairness on the reward side of the equation often stumble on the mistakes and failures side. Many stories that cascade through the organization are about whom to avoid and what businesses or units to avoid. In some companies, even the executives believe "One mistake and you're out."

Such rules of thumb are ordinarily only partially true. One corporation in our study is exceedingly tolerant of thoughtful mistakes because it is embedded in a high-risk environment where fast action is a must. The company also takes a "gentlemen don't tell" attitude toward mistakes made, so that when managers are fired for incompetence, what may be their fifth major mistake appears to observers to be their first. In this case, perception rules truth, and most managers firmly believe "I have to take risks, but I'm dead if I make a big mistake. What I'm asked to do is incongruous."

Incongruity is a problem organizations create for themselves. Not articulating a careful position on mistakes and failures can lead to myths, to managers who are terrified of taking risks, and to managers who cover up and explain mistakes away.

It is nearly always the immediate boss who passes on the organization's attitude toward mistakes. But because bosses each have a uniquely personal response to mistakes, this is akin to handing out shotguns randomly loaded with either buckshot or flowers. For every story of a boss helping a subordinate to learn from mistakes, there is one of a boss who cruelly metes out punishment and scorn. Yet an organization's position on mistakes needs to be as thoroughly consistent and as contingency-based as does its compensation system. Bosses will administer a goof system whether it is articulated or not, and subordinates will analyze the meaning of the boss's actions just as carefully as they scrutinize their paychecks.

A business mistake seemed to matter to the executives we studied for two reasons: It taught them something enduring about how their organizations and their bosses treated mistakes and failures, and it taught them something equally important about their personal shortcomings. What the executives learned about their organizations was not consistent, because most of these events were idiosyncratically dominated by bosses. In the same organization, for example, where one manager was hammered for overspending his authority, another was cheered for even more dramatically overspending his. The conclusion to be drawn is that most organizations provide answers to the question "What happens if I make a big mistake?" But the answers are left to chance and to bosses and to corporate policies that have unintended consequences.

On the personal side, business failures and mistakes were important perhaps because managers had forgotten to do something they already knew how to do. They forgot the most obvious aspect of management—that it is an interpersonal medium.

Hardships

Their mistakes cannot be chalked up to youthful naïveté—the average age at which these mistakes occurred was thirty-six, a time when the majority of the managers were far beyond their first brushes with management. They had been arrogant or insensitive or simply ignored the obvious. That the event reminded them of their shortcomings seems to account for its power. We believe the reason the managers came down so hard on themselves was that there was little excuse for their actions. And perhaps what they learned was not really that other people matter, because more than likely they already knew that. They had simply, in their own haste, proved themselves flawed. When the turmoil subsided and they had a chance to reflect, the lesson of this event may finally have been simple humility. (See figure 4–4 for a summary of the lessons of business mistakes.)

Problem Subordinates

Firing a subordinate, even one who deserves it, is among the most dreaded of management acts. Objectively speaking, the procedure is straightforward: Tell them where they stand, give them a fair chance to improve, then let them go if they don't.

The executives we interviewed were particularly adamant that even an inept subordinate should be given room to save face: Criticize the performance, not the person, who may have all kinds of other talents. If subordinates couldn't or wouldn't accept that they were poor performers, beating them with the facts was cruel. One executive summed up the general opinion by saying:

> If you and the employee are in basic disagreement about his ability, you are usually unlikely to resolve this issue by tackling it head on. You prove nothing by winning and even less by losing! Better to explain to the individual that he has a number of useful talents but he is a poor fit with the business, which will hold back his career prospects. This route gets him out (your goal) and salvages his pride.

Individual Lessons

Setting and Implementing Agendas
- Technical/professional skills
- All about the business one is in
- Strategic thinking
- Shouldering full responsibility
- Building and using structure and control systems
- Innovative problem-solving methods

Handling Relationships
- **HANDLING POLITICAL SITUATIONS**
- Getting people to implement solutions
- **WHAT EXECUTIVES ARE LIKE**
- **HOW TO WORK WITH EXECUTIVES**
- Strategies of negotiation
- Dealing with people over whom you have no authority
- **UNDERSTANDING OTHER PEOPLE'S PERSPECTIVES**
- Dealing with conflict
- Directing and motivating subordinates
- **DEVELOPING OTHER PEOPLE**
- Confronting subordinate performance problems
- Managing former bosses and peers

Basic Values
- You can't manage everything all alone
- Sensitivity to the human side of management
- Basic management values

Executive Temperament
- Being tough when necessary
- Self-confidence
- **COPING WITH SITUATIONS BEYOND YOUR CONTROL**
- Persevering through adversity
- Coping with ambiguous situations
- Use (and abuse) of power

Personal Awareness
- **THE BALANCE BETWEEN WORK AND PERSONAL LIFE**
- Knowing what really excites you about work
- **PERSONAL LIMITS AND BLIND SPOTS**

- Taking charge of your career
- Recognizing and seizing opportunities

Major Learning Thrusts

Handling Relationships

The majority of these events involved the failure to take proper account of other people. Managers learned a potpourri of lessons about the consequences of mistreating and/or ignoring others.

Coping with Situations beyond Your Control

As with demotions, and so on, managers sometimes learned the lessons of tenacity and hanging in against the odds.

Personal Limits

Since these mistakes occurred on average when they were quite experienced, some managers learned humility. They were guilty of ignoring the obvious—that relationships are the glue of organizations.

See Esther Lindsey, et al., *Key Events in Executives' Lives,* Technical Report No. 32 (Greensboro, N.C.: Center for Creative Leadership, 1987), 89–103.

Figure 4–4. *The Potential Lessons of Business Failures and Mistakes*

Some managers admitted procrastinating about problem people for as long as two years in an effort to save the dignity of the subordinate. Most of the time, the problem had been inherited from a previous manager or managers. Although the employees were inept or had drinking problems or were technically obsolete, no one had ever confronted them. The problem employee had been passed along for years.

One manager had inherited an autocratic man who ran a huge accounting function with antiquated procedures. The man scoffed at proposed changes, but he had been with the company forty-five years and was hardworking and loyal. Another manager had inherited a production manager who had been given good job appraisals for thirty-five years but who obviously couldn't handle the job. Soon after taking the job, the manager was ordered to fire the man and tell him about his poor performance. It was in such situations that retraining or development was not really an option. The problem person had been shuffled around or placed in a nominal position for too long. He had little credibility with his co-workers, and for one reason or another couldn't or wouldn't recognize the need for change. He didn't fit with his job and the situation was hopeless.

Precisely because the situation was sometimes hopeless, managers saw the subordinates' plight as pathetic. Many of these subordinates had lived in ignorance, not seeing that they were no longer useful or that their presence was destructive to morale and performance. Their co-workers often took up the slack for them and resented it, or they had watched the problem person with substandard work for years and became disgruntled or cynical themselves. The managers often therefore inherited a disenchanted group along with their problem performers.

When managers acted impulsively on the objective merits of the situation, they learned the hard way that they were firing a person, not discarding an old machine. When they agonized over the situation and procrastinated, they were simply repeating the mistakes of their predecessors. The only effective method, then, was to confront the person quickly and humanely, but to do this they had to overcome some feelings of inadequacy and doubt. Why can't I help this person? Isn't there some other way? How much does it matter? What if I'm wrong and this person can turn around? Firing the person was an admission of failure, the chance of making a mistake and perhaps being labeled a gunslinger. But taking such action was the only way to help anyone in the long run. The only certain mistake was to do nothing.

From these painful situations, the managers we studied learned some paradoxical lessons. Humaneness sometimes meant toughness, and firing someone was often a kinder act than keeping them on. "There's no kindness in keeping these people," one said. "If you hang on to them for too long, they get too old to find another job." They also learned some straightforward lessons about when and how to confront, and when not to confront. But paramount were some realizations about human foibles. Particularly in the cases where nothing worked, they remembered the pathos of it more clearly than anything else.

> He was fifty-eight years old and had bounced around for twenty years. He was pompous; no one liked him. He'd been rotated every two years, and Personnel wouldn't touch the problem. My boss wanted to cut overhead; he told the human resource people we were going to fire him, and it was their job to figure out how to do it right. My boss told me, "Fire him at five o'clock Friday, and don't let him come back." I worried about it for days, couldn't sleep. Then Friday came, and he wasn't there.
>
> I panicked, but luckily he came in. When I was about to fire him, I said, "Let's go to Personnel." That was when he told me he couldn't because it was after five o'clock (quitting time). Then I knew I was doing the right thing.

Even "doing the right thing" hurt, and it didn't get any easier. That they were flawed people dealing with flawed people was the central meaning they took away. (See figure 4–5.)

Individual Lessons

Setting and Implementing Agendas
- Technical/professional skills
- All about the business one is in
- Strategic thinking
- Shouldering full responsibility
- Building and using structure and control systems
- Innovative problem-solving methods

Handling Relationships
- Handling political situations
- Getting people to implement solutions
- What executives are like
- How to work with executives
- Strategies of negotiation

(Continued)

Figure 4–5. *The Potential Lessons of Subordinate Performance Problems*

- Dealing with conflict
- Directing and motivating subordinates
- Developing other people
- **CONFRONTING SUBORDINATE PERFORMANCE PROBLEMS**
- Managing former bosses and peers

Basic Values
- You can't manage everything all alone
- **SENSITIVITY TO THE HUMAN SIDE OF MANAGEMENT**
- Basic management values

Executive Temperament
- Being tough when necessary
- Self-confidence
- Coping with situations beyond your control
- Persevering through adversity
- Coping with ambiguous situations
- Use (and abuse) of power

Personal Awareness
- The balance between work and personal life
- Knowing what really excites you about work
- Personal limits and blind spots
- Taking charge of your career
- Recognizing and seizing opportunities

Major Learning Thrusts

Confront and Act

This was a time to avoid either impulse or procrastination. The courage to invest time and energy in confronting the problem was called for in dealing with the mistakes and foibles of others.

Pathos

What seemed to be remembered the longest was the pathos of the situation, that no matter what, empathy was a must.

See Esther Lindsey, et al., *Key Events in Executives' Lives,* Technical Report No. 32 (Greensboro, N.C.: Center for Creative Leadership, 1987), 127–135.

Figure 4–5. (*Continued*)

Hardships

Jargon sometimes springs up to camouflage this most poignant of situations—"outplacement" and "negative personnel decision" are common euphemisms for telling someone eye-to-eye that they can't cut it in their job. What executives seemed to be saying is that to bury the pathos is a terrible mistake, that if you can't empathize with someone losing their job, then perhaps you have no business managing anyone.

The Value of Hard Times

As the summaries in figures 4–6 and 4–7 demonstrate, hardships seem to startle managers into facing themselves, and coming to grips with their own fallibilities can be a turning point in their development. Some of the managers we studied realized their

Hardship	Learning Thrusts
Personal Traumas	Sensitivity to others
	Coping with events beyond one's control
	Recognition of personal limits/the balance between life and work
Demotions/Missed Promotions/Lousy Jobs	Personal limits
	Organizational politics and coping strategies
	What job managers like and dislike
Breaking a Career Rut	Taking charge of your career
Business Failures and Mistakes	Handling relationships
	Coping with situations beyond your control
	Personal limits
Subordinate Performance Problems	Confront and act on people problems
	Pathos of the human condition

Figure 4–6. *Learning from Hardships*

Individual Lessons

Setting and Implementing Agendas
- Technical/professional skills
- All about the business one is in
- Strategic thinking
- Shouldering full responsibility
- Building and using structure and control systems
- Innovative problem-solving methods

Handling Relationships
- HANDLING POLITICAL SITUATIONS
- Getting people to implement solutions
- WHAT EXECUTIVES ARE LIKE
- HOW TO WORK WITH EXECUTIVES
- Strategies of negotiation
- Dealing with people over whom you have no authority
- UNDERSTANDING OTHER PEOPLE'S PERSPECTIVES
- Dealing with conflict
- Directing and motivating subordinates
- DEVELOPING OTHER PEOPLE
- CONFRONTING SUBORDINATE PERFORMANCE PROBLEMS
- Managing former bosses and peers

Basic Values
- You can't manage everything all alone
- SENSITIVITY TO THE HUMAN SIDE OF MANAGEMENT
- Basic management values

Executive Temperament
- Being tough when necessary
- Self-confidence
- COPING WITH SITUATIONS BEYOND YOUR CONTROL
- PERSEVERING THROUGH ADVERSITY
- Coping with ambiguous situations
- USE (AND ABUSE) OF POWER

Personal Awareness
- THE BALANCE BETWEEN WORK AND PERSONAL LIFE
- KNOWING WHAT REALLY EXCITES YOU ABOUT WORK

- **PERSONAL LIMITS AND BLIND SPOTS**
- **TAKING CHARGE OF YOUR CAREER**
- **RECOGNIZING AND SEIZING OPPORTUNITIES**

See Esther Lindsey, et al., *Key Events in Executives' Lives,* Technical Report No. 32 (Greensboro, N.C.: Center for Creative Leadership, 1987).

Figure 4–7. *The Potential Lessons of Hardships*

dependence on other people and gained a healthy respect for what others can contribute. Becoming more aware of their own shortcomings also gave some of the managers a heightened sense of compassion and tolerance for the foibles of others. Some realized they had stopped listening to people, soliciting their support, or showing their gratitude. They learned that they couldn't take others for granted, nor could they get along without them. Some turned that heightened sensitivity into management techniques, such as goal-setting procedures that give subordinates more of a say, or better ways to keep their bosses informed. Sometimes they got reacquainted with their family and revived their love.

Through hardships, executives also learned how to continue pursuing their goals under painful conditions. Many found that their perseverance led to success. Others learned that they could find ways to persevere even when the outcome was uncertain. They endured hardships and, in doing so, built stamina to face other stressful experiences.

But the lessons of hardships are mixed. In this chapter we have focused on the successful survivors of hardships, yet even many of them came away scarred. Some retreated into denial and cynicism, and others limped along. More than with any of the other developmental events, with hardships there are no guarantees. The value they offer is that there is meaning in suffering. Those who struggle through them can emerge with a clearer view of themselves and what is important to them in life. They can gain humility as a tempering agent to the confidence developed from successes. They can learn how to scrape themselves off the floor and go on. They can develop a heightened appreciation for other people and come to understand the flaws of others as reflections of their own flaws. This is the balance that hardships can add to the mixture of seemingly contradictory qualities that distinguish successful executives from the field of hopefuls.

One executive summed up his view on the human dramas he had faced in a saying he carried with him:

> *Resolve to be tender with the young,*
> *Compassionate with the aging,*
> *Sympathetic with the striving,*
> *And tolerant of the weak and the wrong,*
> *Because sometime in your life*
> *You will have been all of these.*[3]

5
Making the Most of Experience

> Aw shucks, I just happened to be at the right place at the right time. It was no big deal. Just another job.
> —Chuck Yeager[1]

Developing leadership ultimately boils down to what a person does with his or her opportunities and abilities. No guarantees, no magic, no formulas. Lots of luck, good and bad. So what are they, really, these lessons of experience?

Tom Wolfe's best-selling book about America's astronauts, compellingly entitled *The Right Stuff*,[2] introduced many of us to test-pilot hero Chuck Yeager. Later on, Yeager in his autobiography discussed the "right stuff" image in a way that would strike a chord with the vast majority of successful executives we talked with:

> Ever since Tom Wolfe's book was published, the question I'm asked most often and which always annoys me is whether or not I think I've got "the right stuff." . . . The question . . . implies that a guy who has the right stuff was born that way. I was born with unusually good eyes and coordination. I was mechanically oriented, understood machines easily. My nature was to stay cool in tight spots. Is that "the right stuff"? All I know is I worked my tail off to learn how to fly, and worked hard at it all the way. And in the end, the one big reason I was better than average as a pilot was because I flew more than anybody else.[3]
>
> Everything about airplanes interested me: how they flew, why they flew, what each could or couldn't do and why. As much as I flew, I was always learning something new.[4]

Excerpts from *Yeager: An Autobiography*, by General Chuck Yeager and Leo Janos. Copyright ©1985 by Yeager, Inc. Reprinted by permission of Bantam Books. All rights reserved.

Unlike Yeager, the executives we studied were not cult heroes. But their stories, like Yeager's, were filled with unexpected turns, a lot of hard work, a little luck, some special talents, and love for what they were doing. There was no single path to success as an executive in a corporation. We found no secret recipes to follow, no big-name schools that routinely stamped out successful executives.

We chose to study executives viewed by their organizations as having the right stuff, a constellation unique to each individual. Their abilities were awesome. Running a large organization is one of the most challenging and complex jobs anyone could undertake, demanding innumerable skills and abilities, as well as philosophies, values, attitudes, motives, and knowledge appropriate to the demands of the situation. No amount of experience could possibly prepare an executive for all the expected requirements, much less the unexpected challenges of these jobs.

What did seem to characterize the successful executives we studied was not their genetic endowment nor even their impressive array of life experience. Rather, as a group, they seemed ready to grab or create opportunities for growth, wise enough not to believe that there's nothing more to learn, and courageous enough to look inside themselves and grapple with their frailties. Not only could they do these things, they also seemed able to do them under the worst possible conditions: handling a crisis when just getting the job done demanded their full attention and all of their energy; when other people, bosses and subordinates alike, were waiting for them to prove themselves; when personal catastrophe struck; when major forces over which they had no control were dictating events; when no one knew what was happening, much less what to do about it; when they were disappointed or frustrated or victimized.

So if there is indeed a right stuff for executives, it may be this extraordinary tenacity in extracting something worthwhile from their experience and in seeking experiences rich in opportunities for growth. Like Yeager, they not only "flew" more than other people, they were also "always learning something new." In short, the closest thing to a prescription we could find was: Make the most of your experiences.

Making the Most of Experience

> "Are you ready, Chuck?" they ask from the mother ship.
> "All set," I reply.
> The release cable pops and we plunge clear.[5]

Fortunately we don't have to settle for a platitude. "Go for it and make the most of it" seems to have meaning in the context of executive development. First and foremost, it puts responsibility for development squarely where it belongs—with the person who wants to lead. As chapter 6 will describe in great detail, the organization can play a substantial role as well, but ultimately it's what we do for ourselves that makes the difference.

Secondly, it raises both the key issues this research has addressed: What it is that one might go for, and what it is one might take from it. The central challenge is to improve the odds that learning will occur. As one executive put it, "Careers aren't laying on the ground waiting for you to pick them up—unless your father is a major stockholder. Don't sit around and bitch if things don't go your way. You've got to take initiative and make things happen." What is true of careers is true of development. The correlation between years of experience and effectiveness as a manager is virtually zero,[6] meaning that just living a long life doesn't guarantee growth.

We asked executives we interviewed what advice they would give to talented young managers who want to develop. Their suggestions were diverse, but they could be boiled down into three basic themes: Take advantage of opportunities, aggressively search for meaning, and know yourself. At first glance, these three notions are deceptively simple. Most of us believe we do them regularly, or could if we chose to do so. Perhaps, but a deeper look at the advice shows that it sounds simpler than it is.

Going for It

What does it mean to "take advantage of every opportunity you have"? One executive put it well: "Be prepared for change. It's the rule, not the exception. Take advantage of it. Seek out expanding, broadening opportunities. Don't look for comfortable jobs that rest on technical skills. You've got to put yourself under pressure." Another warned, "Watch out for complacency." And another advised, "Be flexible in taking jobs and geographic moves. Accept challenges as they come."

The point, of course, was to think about opportunities to change jobs as opportunities to grow. The experiences that successful executives said made lasting developmental differences to them were, at their most basic level, fix-its, starting from scratches, projects, line-to-staff moves, exceptional bosses, and so on. But, as we suggested in the beginning of this book, it's not the assignment per se that has developmental potential; rather, it's what an assignment requires a person to do. Some of the core elements that make a fix-it challenging—turning around a resistant staff, for example—can exist in other kinds of assignments. One might run into a remarkable boss anytime. We are suggesting that any assignment has developmental elements: The real issue is what are they, and what they might teach.

As we have discussed each of the experiences in assignments, bosses, and hardships, we have tried to point out some of the elements that make that particular experience potent.[7] Theoretically, if we had a comprehensive list of these core elements we could look at any job or assignment and make some guesses about the developmental potential it carries with it.

To begin compiling such a list, we analyzed over 1,200 significant experiences, identifying their core elements and eventually boiling them down to eight basic categories. Work continues to identify and measure the developmental core of experience,[8] but we believe that the dimensions that follow provide a useful way of analyzing assignments for their developmental potential.

Dealing with the Boss. The boss is still the boss, even if he's wrong. The inescapable fact of hierarchy is that everyone, even the most talented, reports to someone with significant power over him. If all bosses were "good," there would be little need to learn how to deal with them. But bosses, like the rest of us, come in all shapes and sizes. In a major corporation the diversity in managers is enormous. No matter whether a particular boss

Making the Most of Experience 125

is good, bad, or just mediocre, he or she can have substantial impact on a subordinate's ability to do a job and/or his or her career opportunities. To ignore relationships with bosses is folly. The boss was described as a significant developmental experience when:

- a manager was in a first-time supervisory role or a big-scope job and the boss was supportive and helpful;[9]
- the boss was an ogre and the manager had to learn how to cope effectively with it;[10]
- the boss had an exceptional skill or attribute that the manager could incorporate into his or her own repertoire;
- the boss had a style quite different from the manager's own style, and significant adaptation was required;[11]
- the boss, who had exceptionally good *or* bad qualities, was either promoted or derailed by the organization.

By facing the variety of bosses over a career, a manager had the opportunity to learn how to deal with quite diverse people in authority.

Dealing with the Staff. Like bosses, the subordinates of developing managers come in all shapes and sizes. And, like dealing with competent bosses, dealing with a competent staff may require relatively little development. The most potent learning experiences were reported when:

- the staff was incompetent and/or resistant to the manager's initiatives, and achieving the business objectives required turning the situation around;
- the staff was inexperienced or "green" and the manager had to build a working team from scratch;
- a key member of the staff, usually inherited, had a serious performance problem that had to be corrected or else the person had to be fired;

- the manager became the boss of former peers or older or more experienced employees, or of someone who was formerly his or her own boss;
- key functions on the staff were vacant or held by incompetent people, and the manager had to do their job in addition to his or her own.

Each of these situations required the manager to develop different skills and strategies. There is no one way to direct and motivate that would satisfy all of these demanding situations, and no amount of formal authority would solve the problem. As one manager said, "You can't fire everybody."

Other Significant Relationships. While the boss and the staff obviously occupy center stage for a manager, critical relationships might face a manager at every turn.[12] Essentially every time a manager had to work with types of people he or she had not dealt with before, the learning potential was high. A few of the most potent included:

- presenting to or working with executives at least two levels higher;
- formal negotiations with clients, suppliers, unions, vendors, or government;
- dealing with people from other cultures whose perspectives and cultures were quite different;
- working with joint venture partners whose views diverged from the manager's;
- dealing with/being dependent upon peers or other corporate denizens over whom the manager had no formal authority, often in a situation where there was no obvious reason for them to cooperate (and often reasons that they weren't inclined to);
- working on a team or task force with people representing different functions, specialties, divisions, and/or levels, where achieving the task required cooperation.

Obviously, the list could go on. As with different kinds of bosses and staff, the manager needed to develop different kinds of skills to deal with the different kinds of relationships. Typically the driving elements for learning were that the manager hadn't worked with these kinds of people before and that there was some level of adversity to be overcome—the cooperation necessary to complete a task was not automatic and the manager's formal authority could not assure it. The heart of the matter was that without their cooperation the manager could not succeed at his own assignment.

The Stakes. Potent developmental situations were seldom safe. Executives often said that they learned the most when the stakes were highest. Among the most salient elements that raised the stakes were:

- high visibility with top management, engendered by the importance of the project or assignment to the business;

- tight deadlines, ultimatums ("Turn it around in a year or we'll sell it"), huge financial risks, or sometimes even threats to the survival of the business;

- going against management's preferences or advice or against corporate tradition or procedures (this was often necessary to exploit opportunities, such as opening new markets, trying out new products, risking venture capital);

- going out on a limb—persuading the corporation to back a new idea or venture on the manager's analysis and recommendation, then having to deliver on the promise.

These and other situations were characterized by the importance of the manager's activity to the business and therefore to top management. The pressure to perform was often immense, and often the manager's career was on the line (and maybe the jobs of many others or even the survival of the business itself). Managers had to learn to cope with the pressures, handle the risks, and take effective action in the face of high stress and enormous consequences. Often the situation was made even worse by shortages of resources or inconceivable deadlines or stacked odds. Two things often stood out: Success or failure was evident to everyone, and responsibility for it was clearly on the manager's shoulders.

Adverse Business Conditions. Of course the heart of a manager's job is to run a business or a part of a business, and the challenges thrown up routinely contained immense developmental potential. Markets went sour, suppliers or customers went out of business, competitors pulled off coups, unions went on strike, the economy went berserk, natural resources ran short, technology changed, equipment failed, consumers rebelled. Responding to these and many other situations, especially ones new to the manager, often demanded new learning. Action had to be taken, usually quickly, and usually it had to be novel. Often there was insufficient time to gather all the data one would like, so action was risky—the problem ambiguous, the stakes high.

As if the business challenges weren't enough, adversity that stimulated growth often came over and above running the business per se. It was generated by a context in which running the business took place:

- facilities had to be built or found, sometimes towns had to be constructed;
- foreign governments, often capricious or hostile, had to be handled;
- severe physical hardships might be confronted, that is, working in the Arctic, tornadoes, the dangers of the jungle;
- the social milieu sometimes presented problems, ranging from shortages of skilled labor to social unrest, riots, and persecution;
- the mores of the local culture sometimes ran contrary to the American work ethic, with local traditions and values flying in the face of business practices and ethics. What managers faced ranged from bribery and corruption to the extremes of macho risk takers and of sheer lack of interest in work.

Making the Most of Experience 129

Many of these and other contextual factors were particularly prevalent in foreign assignments, but were not restricted to them. Managers who were sent to geographically distant parts of the United States experienced similar culture shock and adversity. Whatever its source, contextual demands on top of business challenge created potent demands to develop new skills and understanding.

Scope and Scale. The scope of a managerial job, for the manager in it, is relative. But as one takes on responsibility for more and more people, dollars, functions, products, markets, and/or sites, the demands of sheer scale emerge as key developmental forces.[13] What might be effective management when one could get his or her arms around a whole chunk of a business ceases to work as:

- there are too many people to even know their names, much less their skills, abilities, and motivation;
- there are too many geographically spread locations to personally spend much time on site or to know firsthand the details of the situation at each one;
- there are too many different functions, products, businesses, technologies, or markets to have personal expertise in all (or even most) of them;
- ipso facto, subordinates know a lot more about their pieces of the business than their managers do or could.

Particularly for managers who have developed personal leadership skills, changes in scope present countless demands to learn to "lead by remote control." Dependence on others takes on new meaning, as do the symbolic aspects of being the head honcho of a large organization. Hands-on to hands-off (or at most, selective hands-on) drives the learning from this core element.

Missing Trumps. Bridge players know well that even a good hand can be done in by the missing trumps. One element in many of the significant learning experiences was that the managers came into the situation at least "one down." Often it was a knowledge card: The new situation was in some way unfamiliar or, in some cases, totally strange. It may have been a different function, business, product, or technology that the manager knew little or nothing about. The manager may have been too young, or from the "wrong" background for that job (one manager told us that no one ever got that job unless he had a Ph.D. in chemistry; he was the first). "Country boys" in a gray-suit suite, marketers walking into finance, lawyers becoming managers, accountants taking over line operations, high school graduates managing highly specialized technical operations, MBAs on the factory floor; it went with the turf. Added to whatever other challenges faced them was this highly personal one—having to establish or reestablish credibility while learning the new job. Some found themselves in foreign countries unable to speak the language. Almost as difficult was learning computerese or financialese or legalese, knowing that every conversation made the ignorance obvious. Many learned, like the executive quoted in the chapter on assignments, that there was little else to do but admit ignorance, demonstrate some strengths, and set about learning what you needed to know to handle the job.

Starkness of Transition. Many powerful experiences were driven by the degree of change for the individual. People were promoted two or more levels at once or moved into totally new businesses or plucked from years on the line into some abstract, technical staff assignment with no subordinates and no bottom line. Hotshots sometimes got demoted or exiled to less significant jobs or put in the penalty box. Freewheelers got bridled by a new kind of boss. Managers who had developed reputations by fixing broken operations were sent to start one from scratch.

Sometimes the transition was sudden. A chief negotiator died on the plane to the Middle East and his twenty-six-year-old apprentice, along to observe, became the lead man in a million-dollar deal. Bosses died or were fired, and young managers found themselves in charge. One young lawyer, by virtue of being the only person in the legal department who had taken a course in international law, found himself on a team negotiating trade rights with Japan as seasoned executives looked on.

Personal lives unraveled in the midst of tremendous business pressures; companies merged or reorganized, shunting people up or down overnight; scandals emerged, leaving survivors suddenly in charge of the pieces; or plants shut down, leaving the manager with only the echoes of his footsteps.

Stark transitions; sudden, big changes for better or worse.

The eight dimensions provide one way to assess a job opportunity for its developmental potential, or to analyze what might have been learned after completing an assignment. Certainly they don't encompass everything that a job might demand, nor do they specify precisely what should or could be learned from facing these demands. What appears to be true for these dimensions is that they constitute significant learning opportunities. The courage to take them on (or the judgment to know when the challenge is too much) and the wisdom to learn from them are yet another test of the individual.

Motives for Change

Seizing opportunities that provided such challenges was scary enough, but creating change when none is readily available can be even more difficult. Once a job is mastered or gets too comfortable, it may be time to make an opportunity. The executives we talked with consistently became restless after two or three years in a given job. Rather than stagnate, many of them created their own opportunities. Their action ranged from simply discussing the desire to change with their boss to proposing new ventures or volunteering for task forces. When a change wasn't in the cards, some found ways to take on more in their current jobs. They did not assume that their growth was the organization's responsibility.

Overwhelmingly, their motivation for seeking change was to do something challenging, intriguing, exciting, broadening—not just to get promoted at all costs. This is not to say that successful executives weren't ambitious—they certainly were. But they had some perspective on it, best captured by an executive who advised younger managers not "to plan on being president of [the corporation] in five years. Look out for the next two or three." We were frankly surprised that the vast majority of successful executives we talked to never explicitly strived for the top jobs they currently held, much less the very top. Mostly they wanted to do interesting things and to do them well. Promotions were a means to have more interesting things to do and more resources to do them.

Making Sense of Experience: The Search for Meaning

The second piece of advice, "Never stop learning," seems to be almost automatic for successful executives. John Kotter, for example, observed that

> the most effective GMs had careers characterized by almost constant growth in their interpersonal and intellectual skills, in their knowledge of the business and organization, and in their relationships with relevant others.[14]

Bennis and Nanus, in their study of ninety top leaders, documented the same kind of thing:

> Nearly all leaders are highly proficient in learning from experience. Most were able to identify a small number of mentors and key experiences that powerfully shaped their philosophies, personalities, aspirations, and operating styles. And all of them regard themselves as "stretching," "growing," and "breaking new ground."
> . . . leaders have discovered not just how to learn but how to learn *in an organizational context.*[15]

Our executives were no different—their penchant for learning was undeniable. They wanted to know how things worked and why things happened the way they did. The lessons they learned reflected this compulsion in subtle and not so subtle ways. They wanted to know *how* the product was made, *why* the markets worked as they did, what underlying forces drove the business. When other people were involved, they wanted to know how they viewed the world, why they acted as they did, what their "hot buttons" were. Even reports and numbers got the same scrutiny: "Where do these numbers come from? Why are they reported this way? Which two or three drive all the rest?"

Perhaps it's these thousands of little whys and hows and why nots that eventually mount up to major lessons and subsequently to a major advantage. One never knew when a little piece of information, a tiny bit of knowledge, would hold the key to a business move. The same could be said for less tangible things such as politics—understanding how they worked and why could spell the difference in getting a new initiative approved.

Just as assignments, other people, and hardship experiences differ from one another and offer different kinds of lessons, learning from them occurs through different mechanisms. The lessons of assignments, for example, demand the classic, action-oriented, hands-on, doing-it learning pattern. Through trial and error and trial and success, eventually rewarded by achievement in the assignment, managers learned by doing whatever it took to get the job done. If succeeding meant learning about marketing in three weeks, then that's what they did. If it meant learning how to negotiate with a union, they did that, too. Many of the lessons needed for agenda setting, handling relationships, and honing executive temperament seem to be grasped through the action mode.

Trial-and-error learning from assignments is fraught with peril. Caught up in the action, immersed in the demands and challenges, the manager may have no time for reflection. It is easy to presume that if everything comes out all right it was because of what you did (and that all you did was correct). It is in fast-action, high-pressure situations that people are most prone to rely on their already "proven" skills and approaches and put most of their energy into the demands and problems they have seen before. Thus, pulling off a tough assignment may "teach" the manager that he or she can, after all, manage anything.

Exposure to a significant boss, in contrast, required learning at a distance by observing what others were up to. This is a more cognitive and reflective kind of learning, even though managers were, at times, the victims of other people's actions. While the assignments, by virtue of their demands, *forced* people to learn, the positive and negative role models delivered up object lessons that the observer had first to recognize, then interpret, and finally incorporate. But even that was not enough, because actually using what was learned in one's own behavior required yet another step—either modeling the "right" way or avoiding the "unacceptable" way.

The "lessons on a stage" provided by significant other people may be missed (in fact, in several of the companies, role models were virtually *never* mentioned), especially by fast-tracking, highly self-directed managers. Even when the behavior of someone else gets their attention, it is easy to misinterpret what it means—whether the role model is good or bad. It's possible for a young manager who admires his or her boss to become overdependent, resulting in perceptions that the manager is unable to "cut the cord" or lacks independence. Also possible are unrealistic attempts to imitate the admired qualities even if what someone else does doesn't fit with the manager's own style and strengths.

Badly flawed role models, from whom one hopes people learn what not to do, may teach what to do instead. Especially when managers believe these characters are rewarded by the organization, it's easy to conclude that being political is the way to get ahead or that insensitivity is a key to success or that favoritism is the basis of promotion. Such conclusions, of course, result in warped values that, except in warped organizations, can eventually derail a manager.

The lessons of hardships present yet a third type of learning challenge. Like assignments, hardships left nowhere to hide: The manager had to face up to a situation. But unlike assignments, where confrontation was with markets or people or business situations, hardships forced a confrontation with self, a frightening exposure to one's own frailties and even mortality. To learn from it required mucking around in the psyche and coming to grips with fears and shortcomings and inadequacies—the very antithesis of projecting to oneself (and to others) the image of self-confident leadership.

The hardships, too, and perhaps most of all, appear to guard their lessons well. When faced with difficulty, the manager's first layer of defense is sometimes denial—refusing to believe that it really happened or to accept responsibility for what happened. Mistakes, for example, are easily seen as someone else's fault or the mischance of fate; a demotion might be seen as the boss's jealousy or a personal vendetta rather than as an accurate assessment of the manager. In extreme cases, when hardships are traumatic enough, attempts at denial may result in a form of physical or psychological collapse.

A second layer of defense, even if a person does accept some responsibility for the problem, may be a misplaced belief that nothing can be done about it. These feelings of defeat can result in perceptions of personal inadequacy ("I just can't deal with those situations") or cynicism ("This organization is all politics").

The point, of course, is that trial and error, observe-interpret-incorporate, and psychic delving not only are very different ways of learning but also present different pitfalls to negate or misdirect what learning there is. There are no guarantees that specific individuals will learn what they could from specific experiences. We believe, however, that the executives we studied provided clues for the rest of us that might help in digging out meaning. They seemed to have a highly refined ability to learn from experience that consisted of both motives and skills. Because they care deeply, it hurt to make mistakes. So they learned because it would help them solve a problem or make the business work. When they saw that something they didn't know how to do was necessary to "doing better," they were highly motivated to learn it.

But their motivation to learn was not enough. These executives either had or had to develop tangible skills. Learning required them to be quick studies, able to sift through mountains of information and get on top of it in short order. In the chaos of a new assignment, they had to identify the critical pieces and understand them quickly. They had to learn new technologies or markets or businesses on the run, while others watched every decision to see if the newcomer was credible.

Part of being a quick study was their apparent ability to get beneath the surface. Most of them were keen observers of the things happening around them. This was particularly apparent in their dealings with others, where dealing effectively with them required executives to learn about other people's perspectives, motives, and prejudices. By observing them carefully—bosses and subordinates, customers and suppliers, negotiators and regulators—many of the executives found ways to work with them ("You have to walk in his moccasins" was a typical truism). Executives who lacked the ability (or motivation) to observe and understand others beneath the surface often derailed later on because of the inability to work with and through others.

But even being a quick study and an astute people watcher was not always enough. At yet a deeper level, learning from experience required an ability to look inside oneself and deal with one's own feelings and motives. Especially in learning from hardship experiences, it was necessary to "dig into your own mind, get acquainted with it, find out what it really wants, show it what it can't have and why, and strike a healthy bargain with it on the basis of what is possible."[16] Inability to relate experience to what lies inside oneself severely restricts the ability to learn. Experiences that confront us with our own shortcomings can teach only if we've come to grips with our defenses against them. This leads logically enough to the third piece of advice from these successful executives: "Know yourself."

A Clear Sense of Self

Most people believe they do know themselves, but there is overwhelming evidence from psychological research that a lot of energy is expended protecting our self-image. As easy as it sounds, it can be incredibly difficult to accept knowledge of personal limits, to accept responsibility for mistakes, or to recognize skill deficiencies. And as difficult as accepting the bad news is, it can be even more difficult to do anything about it. Though they sound simple, the basic steps are tough: Seek out feedback from

Making the Most of Experience

others, reflect on what you're doing (especially when things go wrong), be honest with yourself about yourself, and don't let success go to your head. As one executive observed, "There is always someone out there who's smarter than you or knows more about something than you do."

Clearly many of the executives we interviewed faced their shortcomings because of a crisis—they were demoted or fouled up or ran into an intolerable boss or otherwise were essentially forced to confront themselves. But more fundamentally, many of them seemed to have a mind-set about themselves that allowed them to face their flaws. They seemed pragmatic about their own shortcomings, perhaps because of two characteristics they shared widely: (1) sufficient self-confidence, born of prior success in tough situations, to feel comfortable with having proved real strengths, and (2) sufficient desire to succeed at the job to actively seek knowledge that would help them do better. Healthy self-confidence in their own abilities made it easier to accept flaws in some areas. Desire to do the job better drove them to view flaws or weak spots as opportunities to improve their performance rather than as personal indictments.

Our findings and inferences mesh well with Bennis and Nanus, who observed that the ninety leaders they studied had a healthy sense of self. They noted:

> It may be easier to say what positive self-regard isn't than what it is. To begin with, it is not a crowing self-importance or egoistic self-centeredness . . . nor is it what's ordinarily meant by a "narcissistic character." There was no trace of self-worship or cockiness in our leaders. But they knew their worth. They trust themselves without letting their ego or image get in the way.[17]

A Framework for Development

The discussion so far about seizing opportunities, digging for meaning, and understanding one's self sets the stage for personal change. It may be useful to look at development as a series of choices: a choice to put one's self in situations that will expose shortcomings and demand new learning; a choice to accept responsibility for one's shortcomings and for the learning; and a choice to do something about it. (These choices are summarized in figure 5–1.)

In the next chapter we will discuss at some length what organizations can do to promote development, but for now we reiterate the theme of this chapter: Ultimately we are each responsible for our own development. The figure outlines that theme, beginning with a choice we make to expose ourselves or to avoid new situations. Most of the executives we studied chose the proactive pathway, accepting or pursuing challenging new situations and learning about themselves one way or another.

The first choice also suggests that the option to active pursuit (at least for managers with any hope of rising in the hierarchy) is not avoiding risk but waiting for something to happen. In short, shortcomings will be revealed one way or another, and when they are, we face the second choice: to deny them or to accept responsibility and try to understand them.

The figure suggests that the diagnosis may reveal a lack of knowledge, experience, or skills—all of which can be changed—or a more difficult change situation rooted in basic personality, ability, or the job itself. Neither diagnosis prohibits change, but, as we shall see, the strategies one chooses to deal with shortcomings are influenced by the ease with which they can be changed and the degree of personal commitment to the change.

In the end, development boils down to the same "do it, fix it, try it" philosophy found in excellent companies.[18] Awareness of a flat side, coupled with an understanding of it, opens the door to change. Conventional wisdom would suggest changing one's self by building on existing strengths and correcting weaknesses. Our experience with talented executives suggests a slightly different approach, one which emphasizes building new strengths, finding ways to compensate for weaknesses, and anticipating situations in which weaknesses or lack of a strength might be fatal.

Building or Discovering New Strengths

Whether in a corporation or on a baseball team, problems often begin when specialists become managers. But being a top-notch

```
┌─────────────────────────────────────────────────────────────────────┐
│                 Choice: Finding Out about Shortcomings  ◄──► Avoid  │
└─────────────────────────────────────────────────────────────────────┘
```

```
       ╱                                          ╲
wait for a catastrophe to         or      actively pursue an accurate
reveal weaknesses                         portrait of self
```

- sooner or later: a big mistake
- sooner or later: a missed promotion, negative appraisal, demotion, or termination

- jump into new situations
- dig for information
- seek feedback from others
- introspect

```
┌─────────────────────────────────────────────┐
│      Choice: Accepting Responsibility       │ ◄──► Deny
└─────────────────────────────────────────────┘
                       │
              Diagnosis of Shortcomings
                  ╱              ╲
         Result of:       or     Result of:
         lack of knowledge       personality
         lack of experience      limited ability
         lack of skills          situational misfit
```

```
┌─────────────────────────────────────────────┐
│         Choice: What to Do about It         │ ◄──► Ignore
└─────────────────────────────────────────────┘
```

Build New Strengths	Anticipate Situations	Compensate	Change Self
○ find situations where learning new things is essential ○ find ways to get help and support while learning	○ ask "dumb" questions ○ seek advice, counsel ○ spend time learning ○ use others' expertise	○ avoid certain situations ○ delegate to others ○ choose staff who cover weaknesses ○ change the situation	○ intensive counseling, coaching ○ personal change effort ○ change just enough to get by

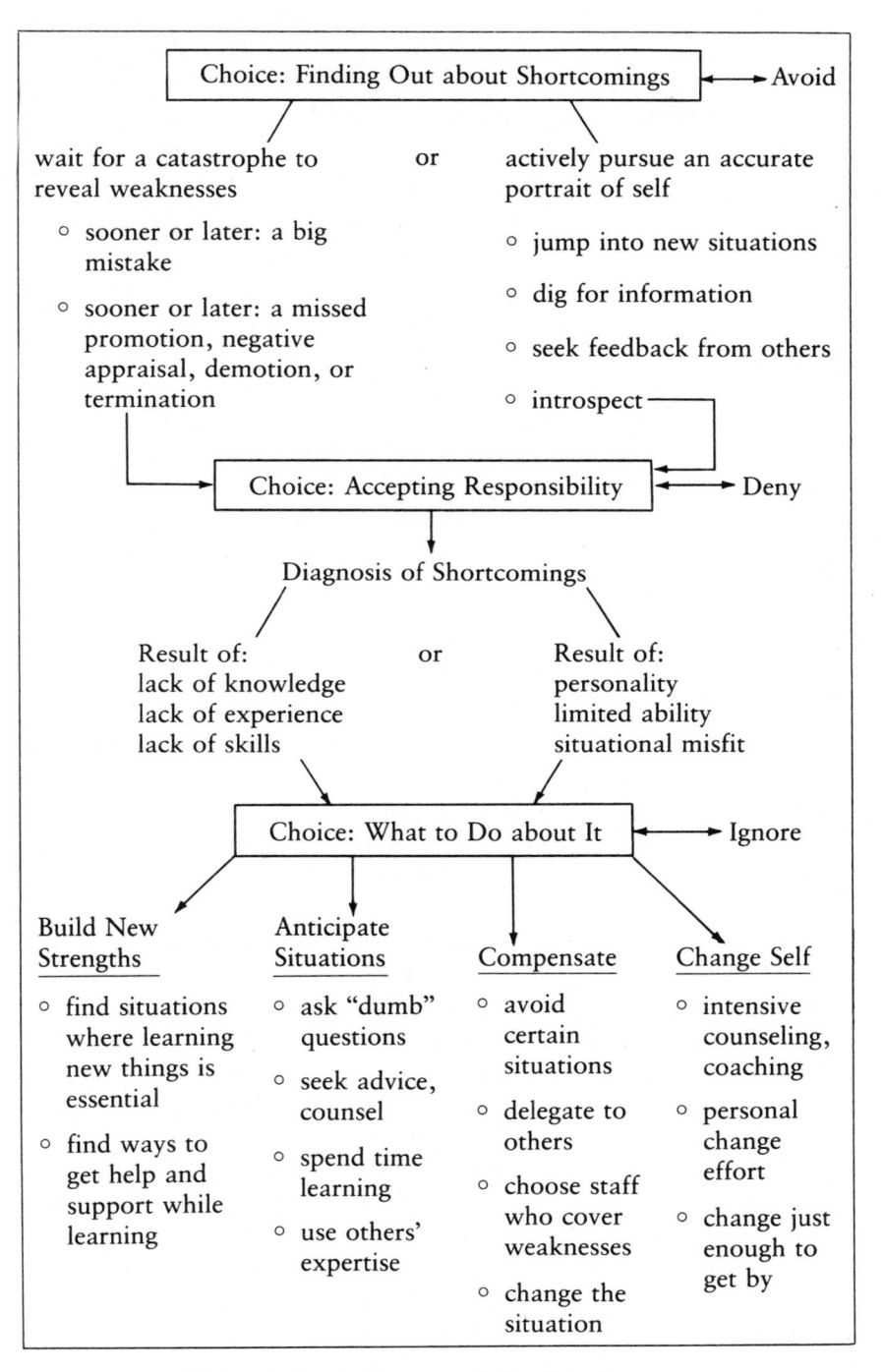

Figure 5–1. *A Framework for Development*

engineer does not guarantee managerial skills any more than a good shortstop is de facto a good coach. It would seem that talented people rather naturally practice and improve upon their existing skills. For management, however, the challenge is not just broadening specialist skills; it's building entirely new skills as the original strengths grow less relevant. As one looks at the lessons listed throughout this book, it's obvious that many of them are unique to the managerial job. Unless there is an as yet undiscovered chromosome, such skills must be developed.

The question, of course, is how to go about it. The answer lies in the dominant theme of this book—seeking out the kinds of experiences that offer something new. It is never easy to leave the security of something one already does well for the uncertainty of the new, but the willingness to take a risk is the precursor of building new strengths.

Compensating for Weaknesses

Self-help books fill the bookstores, offering creative advice for innumerable problems—obesity, smoking, delinquent kids, you name it. The collective message is that you can and should fix whatever ails you. This is probably good advice, but we noticed that many of the executives we met had not declared war on their downsides. Instead, they tended to find ways to compensate for their weaknesses.[19] One executive vice-president, for example, declared "I'm not good with details. I can't stand detail. But I'm damn sure I have someone on my staff who relishes it."

We see a substantial difference between being unaware of weaknesses and being aware of them but choosing to live with them. So awareness is a prerequisite. Then comes the decision to undertake radical surgery, take two aspirins, or find ways to make the malady less harmful. The possibility of achieving fundamental change in adult personality is a matter of debate. The evidence for major change even as a result of intensive therapy is, to put it generously, mixed. Improving specific skills—for example, public speaking—is a possibility. How to deal with a weakness seems to depend on the answers to several questions: How much does the weakness get in the way, now and in the

Making the Most of Experience

context of future jobs? How hard would it be to achieve noticeable improvement? Are there ways to cover for the weakness?

Because successful executives are demonstrably talented, they have both self-confidence and real strengths. They have achieved their success in spite of their weaknesses, and more than one told us they feared messing around with their style. As we saw in an earlier chapter, it often took a real hardship to motivate serious self-correction. Given this state of affairs, compensation strategies coupled with modest correction of weaknesses seems a reasonable approach, unless the flaw is quite critical. Some examples we have run into include:

Weakness	Examples of Compensatory Action
Inattentive to detail	Hire staff person who relishes detail
Inarticulate at presenting	Hire speechwriter
	Use professional graphics
	Well-written documents (in place of speech or as supplement)
	Delegate or share presentations
	Keep them short
Unable to resolve conflict	Avoid settings where conflict flares
	Find substitute to handle that person
	Keep it professional
Proclivity to overmanage subordinates	Engineer geographic separation
	Take on challenging task that demands a lot of time
	Set up reporting system to satisfy compulsion without hands-on intervention
	Take vacation at critical time
Tactical orientation at expense of strategic view	Participative decision making on strategy
	Schedule presentations (up or down) to force thinking
	Delegate tactical issues
	Schedule strategic brainstorming sessions

Compensation strategies are not purposefully corrective. While some of them (for example, participative strategy sessions) may result in changed behavior and thinking, the primary impact is in counterbalancing weaknesses. The philosophy is that "this is a problem that I can't or won't do something about, but I will take some steps to reduce its negative effects." If people will not or cannot change themselves, compensation focuses them on things they can change: their behavior and the situations that shape their behavior.

Anticipating Situations

The stories of these executives were stories of change—constant, often unpredictable, often dramatic. Either because they focused on what they already did well or because they were overconfident in their skills, executives sometimes learned the hard way from many of the transitions. This is not a bad way to learn, but it's not always necessary. "I forgot to sell my boss on the idea." "I thought I had all the answers and I was going to show them how it should be done." "I didn't want them to see how little I knew about the business, so I didn't ask questions." "I quickly discovered I couldn't fire everyone." "I totally reorganized marketing because I knew how to do that. Unfortunately, that wasn't the problem."

Executives we interviewed survived the surprises and learned from them. Many executives we didn't interview, those described as derailed, were less fortunate. When bosses changed, when executives changed jobs, and when reorganizations shook things up were all times when flaws popped out. Handling major transitions appears to be a critical issue,[20] and anticipating what aspects of a new situation will play to one's weaknesses or test the untested may make all the difference. Often it was not bad business decisions alone that did people in. It was such things as a boss with a very different style, a staff that was resistant (or more experienced than the manager), a difficult relationship with a peer or partner or union, and how one handled areas he now had to manage but knew little about.

In short, the same kinds of things that create opportunities for learning and growth can create career threats. Anticipating them not only reduces the possibility of big mistakes but also enhances the likelihood that confronting them will result in learning.

Diversity and Balance: Goals of Development

Diversity of experience and balance in the lessons learned—these were the repeated themes from the careers of these successful executives. Diversity in exposure to developmental assignments, significant bosses, and hardships, over time, is one of the guidelines for development. Diversity brings changes in the kinds of challenges to be met and the types of adversity to be overcome. That is what we believe sets the stage for learning and growth, not just for executives but for all of us. Bronowski perhaps said it best:

> We have to understand that the world can only be grasped by action, not by contemplation. . . . The most powerful drive in the ascent of man is his pleasure in his own skill. He loves to do what he does well and, having done it well, he loves to do it better.[21]

But diversity alone is only part of the story. Exposure to potent experiences does not guarantee that a person will learn something from it. Different experiences can teach different things, so what a person learns depends heavily upon which opportunities that person has. In addition to diversity, one hopes to see balance in the lessons learned over time.

In a simple world, people are blandly unidimensional. The good ones possess all the virtues; the bad monopolize the vices. But the world is not simple, and effective leaders are hardly unidimensional. Douglas MacArthur, described by William Manchester as "unquestionably . . . the most gifted man-at-arms this nation has produced," was no unidimensional soul:

> He was a great thundering paradox of a man, noble and ignoble, inspiring and outrageous, arrogant and shy, the best of men and the worst of men, the most protean, most ridiculous, and most

sublime. . . . Flamboyant, impervious, and apocalyptic, he . . . could not acknowledge errors, and tried to cover up his mistakes with sly, childish tricks. Yet he was endowed with great personal charm, a will of iron, and a soaring intellect.

For every MacArthur strength there was a corresponding MacArthur weakness.[22]

We contend that all of us, executives included, are a little like MacArthur. We are contradictory, paradoxical, and miscellaneous jumbles of vices and virtues. And this is why balance is so basic. Every strength can also turn out to be a weakness, and great strengths or weaknesses can grow unjustifiably overblown. The issue is the particular combination of strengths and weaknesses a person brings to a particular situation. For executives, these balances often appear to be basic contradictions, surfaced by contradictory demands of the job:

- acting alone *and* working with others
- making tough decisions *and* treating people with compassion
- having the confidence to act *and* the humility to know there are other views
- seizing opportunities *and* planning for the future
- taking control *and* accepting the inevitable
- persevering in the face of adversity, yet changing direction when you're wrong

So balance is not a scorecard of lessons, with two checked in every column. Balance is not something attained all at once and then owned forever. As we mean it, balance reflects fundamental tensions that, over the years, get out of whack. When something gets unbalanced, we have to learn in order to get it back under control.

Models imply stasis, so we are tempted to avoid them. Nonetheless, what executives told us can be visualized as in figure 5–2. In essence, it suggests the following picture of development:

Making the Most of Experience

```
Assignments                                    Hardships

         Confidence          Humility
         Independence        Perspective
         Knowledge
         Relationships
         Toughness


                    Values
                    Politics


                    Bosses
```

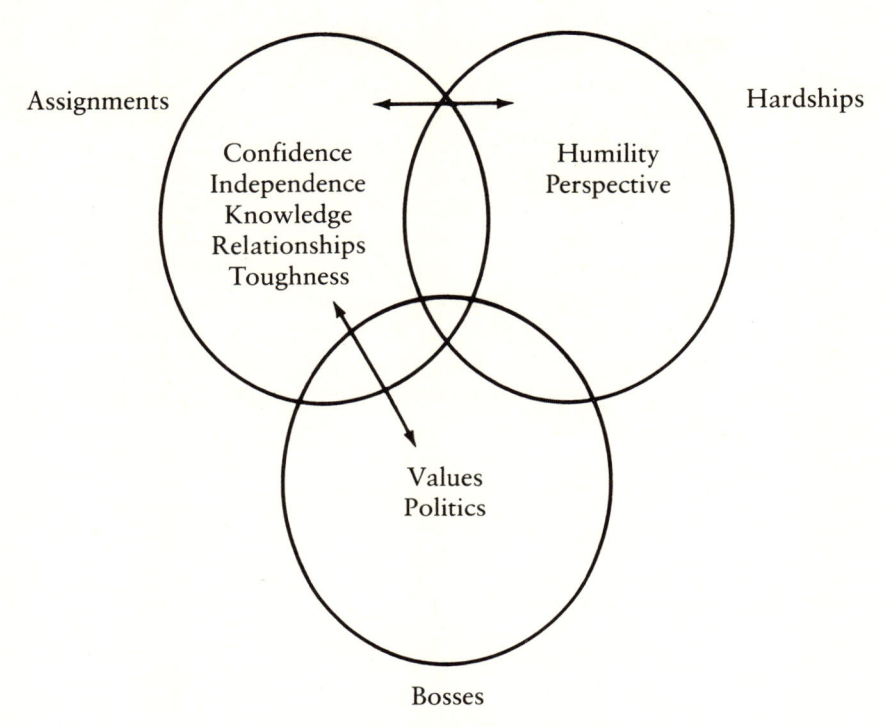

Figure 5-2. *Balance*

1. Different experiences offer to teach different lessons. Assignments are a primary source of independence, knowledge of the business, confidence, leadership, toughness, handling relationships. Bosses are a primary source of managerial and human values and lessons of politics. Hardships expose personal limits and perspective on self.

2. Diversity in experiences provides exposure to diverse lessons. Diversity in lessons learned can lead to balance. The confidence spawned by success in tough assignments may need the balance engendered by a hardship that confronts a manager with his or her limits. Toughness may evolve into insensitivity if not balanced by basic values around the treatment of others.

The Right Stuff

Nor was there a test to show whether or not a pilot had this righteous quality. There was, instead, a seemingly infinite series of tests. A career in flying was like climbing one of those ancient Babylonian pyramids made up of a dizzy progression of steps and ledges, a ziggurat, a pyramid extraordinarily high and steep; and the idea was to prove at every foot of the way up that pyramid that you were one of the elected and anointed ones who had the right stuff and could move higher and higher and even—ultimately, God willing, one day—that you might be able to join that special few at the very top, that elite who had the capacity to bring tears to men's eyes, the very Brotherhood of the Right Stuff itself.[23]

Excerpt from *The Right Stuff* by Tom Wolfe. Copyright © 1979 by Tom Wolfe. Reprinted by permission of Farrar, Straus and Giroux, Inc.

6
Making It Work: The Corporate Opportunity

In a recent conversation, the chief executive of a major corporation made evident his exasperation about executive development:

> I'm not sure what the term means. What is management development anyway? Is it a bunch of systems? I don't think so, but I can't get a straight answer. What's the vision behind it?

Management development is viewed all too often as a bagful of devices: career path planning, human resource planning, mentoring programs, rotational systems, developmental plans on the appraisal form, training courses, education centers, early identification programs. It is, instead, an organization's conscious effort to provide its managers (and potential managers) with opportunities to learn, grow, and change, in hopes of producing over the long term a cadre of managers with the skills necessary to function effectively in that organization. Within that verbose definition, notice the following implications:

1. Development is organizationally specific. The aim is to help people develop to function more effectively in a specific organizational context.
2. Development is part of a long-term business plan. The reason for development is to insure that the quality of manage-

ment is up to the task of getting the organization where it wants to go. While education may be valuable in its own right, development is a good investment only if, over time, it yields more effective managers.

3. Development involves providing opportunities. There clearly are no guarantees that specific individuals will make anything of those opportunities, but without them there can be no development.

4. Development is a conscious effort. Clearly much development occurs by chance. What differentiates an organization that tries to develop managers from one that does not is a clear priority for, and some means of ensuring, developmental opportunities for its best people.

If these statements are true, then the beginnings of a workable management development approach lie first of all in the organization itself—its culture and its business strategy. The belief in development must permeate the culture. The priority must be clear, and the actions of the organization must be consistent with the priority. If development is an extra, an option, a luxury, if no one is held accountable for it, if it disappears every time the business hits tough going, then it isn't likely to thrive. And because it is a long-term proposition, the business itself must be stable enough both to create the culture and to allow its manifestations to play out over time as measured by careers. So the first question, long before we worry about "how," is whether it's feasible to undertake a serious management development effort. Based on our work with corporations that are struggling with such issues, there are four questions that can shed light on how ready an organization is to get serious about executive development. Does the organization have strong corporate identity, or is it a conglomerate with many independent parts? Is the corporation willing to take developmental risks, risks that can be expensive? Is the culture of the organization supportive of learning, encouraging people to try new things and supporting them when they screw up? Is the organization willing to identify and monitor a pool of promising talent, even though it may create elitism?

Corporation or Conglomerate?

> We aren't worried about management development. We buy and sell companies. If management's no good, we sell it.

This statement by a senior vice-president in a large conglomerate makes the point clearly. A corporation that defines itself as a highly diversified conglomerate or a holding company, acquiring or divesting businesses on financial grounds, is hardly in a position to effectively cultivate top-level executive talent. If it happens at all, it would be within the various businesses. At the other extreme, a corporation with a strong corporate (as opposed to subunit) identity is in a better position to move people across functional and business boundaries, to benefit from broad exposure and perspective, and to build diversity into the experiences of managers over their careers.

We learned from our study that each organization was different. Each had its own distinct profile of developmental experiences and a top executive pool with different patterns of strengths and weaknesses. Many conglomerates are little more than clusters of separate businesses, with their own cultures, values, practices, and experiences loosely hung together by a corporate office. If the businesses are sufficiently diverse, it's not clear what advantage rotation across them may yield, even if it were possible to leap the castle walls.

Organizations aren't all one way or another, of course. The diversification binge of the seventies and the takeover craze of the eighties have left many companies in a strange sort of hybrid state. Neither fish nor fowl, they are left to struggle with multiple personalities or unified identities forged at best by high-level abstractions ("All of our businesses involve technology"). Simplified graphics (figure 6–1) make the point.

Peters and Waterman argued that the excellent companies "stick to the knitting," meaning that they have a common business across their parts, common values, and integrated goals.[1] Organizations that effectively develop executive talent seem to share these characteristics. In companies with strong identities

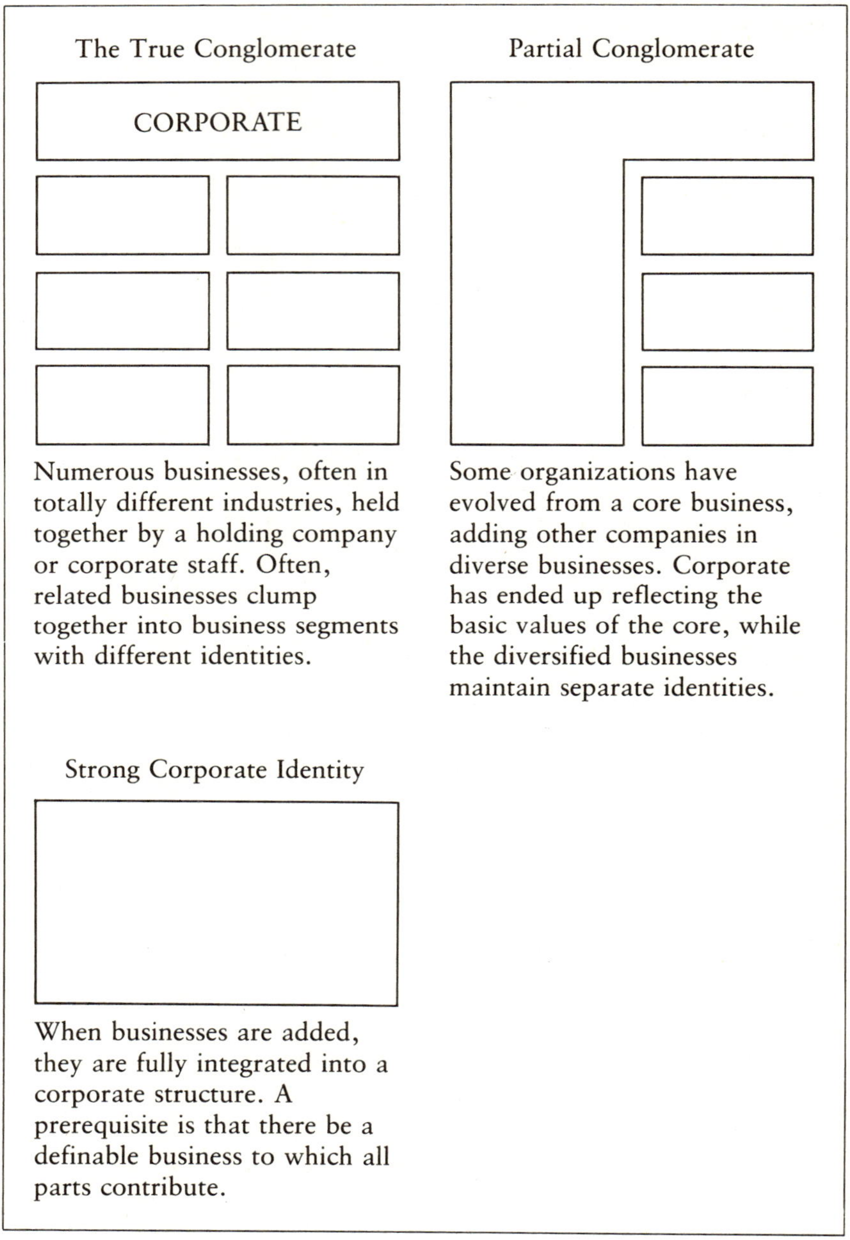

The True Conglomerate

CORPORATE

Numerous businesses, often in totally different industries, held together by a holding company or corporate staff. Often, related businesses clump together into business segments with different identities.

Partial Conglomerate

Some organizations have evolved from a core business, adding other companies in diverse businesses. Corporate has ended up reflecting the basic values of the core, while the diversified businesses maintain separate identities.

Strong Corporate Identity

When businesses are added, they are fully integrated into a corporate structure. A prerequisite is that there be a definable business to which all parts contribute.

Figure 6–1. *Corporation or Conglomerate?*

across businesses, we more frequently find consensus on the priority of management development, identification by managers with a corporate entity and the concomitant willingness to move across business (and even line/staff) boundaries, and a commitment to developing executive talent from within.

Even if corporate identity is weak, strong identities within business units can form a foundation for development. The same strategies can be enacted within the specific businesses or business segments of the most highly diversified holding company. Developmentally, though, these businesses are operating independently, as if there were no others. The perspectives of the executives tend to be myopic, focused on their own part of the business, and they carry with them the values and styles of that part. One might argue that a top management committee, if drawn from the diverse businesses, would have an advantage because of the diversity, and as a team would provide the needed corporate perspective. Our experience suggests otherwise. Myopia carries into the executive suite, and many conglomerates end up hiring their top-level people from the outside. Recent research indicates, however, that hiring outsiders at the top can be a risky business.[2]

Our conclusion, then, is that a large organization's capacity to develop executive talent begins with its fundamental self-definition and strategy. When there is no strong corporate identity, resources might be better spent on selection rather than development, with the latter left up to decentralized business units. When there is a corporate identity, with integration of businesses and common goals, developing executive talent becomes a more feasible proposition. In short, developing executives is, in our view, a business strategy. It is dependent on knowing what business one is in.

Developmental Risks

> We are a bottom-line, performance-oriented company. If you don't get the numbers, you're in deep trouble. I am very conservative when I choose people for key jobs. . . . I won't put someone in there unless I'm real sure they can do it.

The issue of risk is highlighted by this executive vice-president's response to a question on when he would take a developmental risk—assigning a person to a job because he or she might develop in it, rather than choosing the "best qualified" (that is, someone who has already demonstrated that he or she can handle it). Our work suggests that the best-qualified candidates may in fact develop the least, because they've already learned the basic lessons of the experience by virtue of doing it before. It is in this choice that selection versus development clashes most dramatically, and it surfaces directly the issue of what it means to invest in development. An executive who fails or makes numerous mistakes while learning costs the company money. At higher levels, the stakes can run into millions of dollars.

Ironically, most companies view developmental costs in terms of the investment they make in training activities, human resource staff, and related, identifiable activities (for example, building a training center). While such investments are sometimes staggering, we suggest the index of commitment to development is in the bottom line, and far more expensive than it appears. As one executive put it in response to the question about taking a developmental risk:

> I assigned him to that job because I thought he would learn from it. He clearly wasn't the most qualified candidate. I figured if he couldn't cut it, it would cost us two million. In a two-billion-dollar business, we could afford it.

In some large corporations, the entire training and development budget isn't $2 million! And this risk was for one high-potential executive.

The willingness to invest in development takes other shapes. As we've worked with more and more corporations, we've accumulated specific examples of direct investment in development through on-the-job experience:

- venture capital pools for high-potential managers to start up new things

- buying and holding onto small (and often low margin) businesses so young managers can manage a whole business (P&L responsibility)
- creating staff and "assistant to" jobs so line managers can be exposed to corporate staff and/or high-level executives
- hanging onto businesses in trouble so managers can have a shot at turn-around situations
- investing in project teams and task forces to give high-potential managers experience in acquisitions, joint ventures, new product or market development, and so on
- continuing top salaries so high-potential managers will take certain jobs that normally pay less but provide needed experience or exposure.

It is clear that development via experience can be an expensive proposition. Corporations that are risk averse in a business sense may be risk averse developmentally as well. But whether the risks are higher with or without development depends on one's perspective. In the short term, the costs appear high. But Kotter's study of well-managed firms documented their use of these kinds of developmental opportunities.[3] Our own study of derailed executives suggests that while the cost of such risks may be high, not taking risks may be costlier still.[4]

Developing executive talent requires a corporate commitment to risk. This translates into a willingness to invest in creating developmentally valuable learning experiences, perhaps accepting suboptimal business returns for the sake of learning. It does not mean fiscal irresponsibility, but it does suggest additional parameters when viewing return on investment. In its essence, it boils down to this: When asked when they would take a developmental risk in assigning a high-potential person to a job, executives responded that they take *reasonable* chances. We remind you of the story we recounted earlier about the manager who made a mistake that cost the company $100,000. Plagued by guilt, he suggested to his boss that maybe he should be fired.

His boss's response? "Why should I fire you when I've just invested $100,000 in your development?"

Some executives think there is no choice but to take risks in the development of talent. As one observed, "If I promote someone who has absolutely proven he or she can handle the new job, then I am not promoting them, since there is no development involved. And this strategy can't work anyway. The best people will have already left the company by this point."

A Culture to Support Learning

Investing in on-the-job experience makes sense, whether the organization is inclined toward rigorous selection ("Let's see if he can do it") or toward development ("Let's put him in there so he can learn about acquisitions"). The difference between a hard-nosed, survival-of-the-fittest philosophy and one of development lies in the support systems available and in the reactions to inevitable mistakes. The need for support arises from the assumption that while development is primarily a manager's own responsibility, it is exceedingly difficult to do it alone. And, obviously, intolerance of mistakes can stop development in its tracks.

What does it mean to support development? Again, the best definition may lie in examples of what some corporations and some managers *do,* rather than in abstract philosophy.

- Explaining why a person is being given a certain assignment, especially if it may be seen as an undesirable or lateral move. As we noted earlier, we were told many stories of transfers that were intended as developmental but seen as a demotion or banishment by the person involved. Much was learned, but little was what the company had hoped. Knowing why one is being assigned to this job, what it is hoped will be learned, and what will happen next can make all the difference.

- Avoiding unnecessarily stacking the deck. Sending a high-potential manager who knows nothing about marketing into a situation with an incompetent marketing staff and a lousy boss may be laying it on a little thick. At a minimum, a journey into the unknown is more developmental when the voyager can access the resources to learn from: an exceptional boss, a highly competent subordinate, access to experts, preparatory courses, or coaching.

- Providing some means of getting feedback or of interpreting feedback. Being "successful" at leading a booming business or "failing" to turn around a total disaster may tell a manager *nothing*. Useful learning lies a level deeper, in *how* one handled the situation at hand, in what use one made of the resources available, in what might have been done differently. Some bosses are good at providing this information. Occasionally some performance appraisals delve deeply enough in a timely manner. But for the most part, it's the manager alone who bears sole responsibility for the autopsy.

- Providing opportunities for growth and encouraging people to accept them. Indeed, we have run across the panoply of experiences described in this book, from the availability of educational experience to various challenging assignments, used deliberately by one organization or another.

The list could go on, but the basic premise is clear. Development, like any major business priority, can happen only when corporate resources are brought to bear consistently toward the objective. Part of that consistency is dealing with the mistakes people make in pursuit of growth. This topic was covered in some depth in chapter 4, but the point bears repeating here. The issue is not whether mistakes are made, but whether anyone learns from them. An organization that does not tolerate mistakes won't have many managers admitting to them or, by definition, learning from them. A developmentally oriented company, on the other hand, will focus on how the person handled the mistake and what was learned from it.

We don't want to imply that the companies we studied were "soft." As one executive put it, "We don't specialize in safety nets." Dumb mistakes, repeated mistakes, are not typically tolerated in any well-managed corporation. Even educational blunders weren't always without punishment. But what did mark the more tolerant companies went beyond a basic value about learning from error to specific actions to make recovery possible. Penalty boxes, demotions, bad appraisals, or even exile might follow, but it was made clear that losses could be regained. The major vehicle for this, of course, was example—people who went down and came back up, people who were given clear feedback, counseled, and given another shot.

The Corporate Resource

> The products belong to the businesses. The people belong to the corporation.

This executive took a clear stance on a tough issue. We don't see an alternative to identifying the most promising talent and nurturing it. As in any other profession, there are relatively few truly exceptional managers. The experiences we have described in this book are also relatively rare. The heart of development is providing the right opportunities to the right people in the context of a coherent business strategy. That it doesn't always happen isn't simply a matter of misguided managers blocking developmental transfers because of functional, product, or business blinders. They sometimes resist making developmental moves for their people because losing their best people hardly helps them run the business—and that's assuming they even know what developmental opportunities exist in other parts of the corporation.

Coming full circle, the more the organization resembles a conglomerate, the less likely development will be viewed beyond the immediate boundaries and talent pool of the independent parts. Somehow, an organization hoping to develop high-potential managers must find a way to overcome the inevitable boundaries to accomplish two things: across the corporation, to identify a manageable pool of talented people and to identify the relevant developmental opportunities for them.

Corporate strategies for these goals range from nonexistent to elaborate formal systems of assessment and placement. Some companies let people know they've been knighted (put on a fast track), while others try to keep it secret. Some devote incredible amounts of time to systematic reviews of high potentials (sometimes lasting three to six months annually), while others handle people piecemeal as jobs open up. Some put high-potential decisions in the hands of strong human resource functions; others empower small committees of line managers to make such decisions. Corporations also vary in how deeply into the ranks they look, some taking a corporate interest from entry level on, others waiting until people reach middle or higher levels. But organizations that are serious about development seem to have something in common: They keep track of their most promising people, one way or another, and deal with the undesirable by-products.

In our opinion, companies that effectively identify and track their high-potential managers do the following:

- They dip deeply. Review procedures ensure that young talent is evaluated, as well as the more seasoned.
- They look widely. Business, product, divisional, and functional boundaries are crossed. It is assumed that top-level talent may reside anywhere.
- They apply common criteria. Comparing people across boundaries means finding some common basis for comparison. How does one compare a marketing wizard to a financial wizard, or tell if either has general manager potential? There is no clear answer, but the better companies focus on managerial talents rather than on specialist skills.
- They reassess frequently. Being in the high-potential pool is not a free ride. Means are found to allow new people in and get the disappointments out.
- They bring a corporatewide perspective to bear. Whoever is doing the assessing, whether from human resources or line executives, they have a broader perspective. A committee, for example, might contain people from various businesses and staff functions or be comprised of managers with multiple perspectives across the business.

In our experience, corporations are much less proficient at identifying developmental experiences than they are at defining a talent pool. It is not unusual to find firms whose top executives will have "gone through the chairs," meaning that they have held a certain string of positions considered important to development. Nor is it unusual to find companies that use rotation (exposure to various parts of the business) or mentors (exposure to influential managers) or career pathing (plotting exposure according to a hypothetical sequence of important jobs). As we will discuss shortly, however, these strategies seem to miss the important developmental key that it's what one has to face in the job, not the job per se, that matters. Exposure to job content is not so much the issue as what one has to do while being exposed. We believe that more effective development systems target broad types of managerial challenges that provide specific exposure developmentally. For example, it might be desirable for a corporate officer over a career to have:

- had multifunctional P&L responsibility (maybe in an overseas assignment or through running a small business);
- served some time on corporate staff in a strategy or financial role (or in the line, if most of the career was staff);
- served on a task force that solved a major corporate problem germane to the business strategy (for example, opened a new market, developed a new product, or handled an acquisition);
- managed a business in deep trouble and turned it around.

These and the other experiences described earlier in this book represent distinct challenges, not diversity for its own sake.

Foundations of Development

When I was brought in [from the outside], there wasn't a single person inside the company with enough breadth to do my job, or even the jobs reporting to me. That'll never happen here again.

Making It Work 159

It's a long jump between the commitment expressed by this senior executive and achieving the objective. We believe that the process begins in the very nature of the organization, that there are certain soils in which the seeds of development are more likely to root. Figure 6-2 summarizes our view. To the extent that an organization has a strong identity around which its various parts can unite, is willing to invest substantial sums for development on the job (taking a risk), has a culture supportive of development and tolerant of mistakes, and views its most promising talent as a corporate resource, the probability increases that a meaningful developmental effort can be sustained.

Building Block	Advantages	Disadvantages
Strong corporate identity	Managers more willing to cross boundaries	Loss of autonomy of business units
	Assignments across the organization available for development	Loss of esprit that may exist in certain businesses (especially acquired)
	Business goals coherent enough to guide developmental strategy	Loss of diversity, individuality across the business
Willingness to take risks	Puts talent in jobs on basis of developmental goals	Cost of hanging on to low margin or unprofitable businesses
	Increases breadth of developmental opportunities available	Alienation of solid performers who see themselves as more qualified
	Encourages executives to take chances, discover talent	Costly errors as people learn

(Continued)

Figure 6-2. *Some Pros and Cons of a Strong Foundation for Development*

Building Block	Advantages	Disadvantages
Supportive culture	Feedback-rich environment—focused on how one went about it, rather than what was achieved Encourages people to take risks, make mistakes—if they learn from them Provides counsel, assistance, resources	Short-term objectives may not be met Danger of overtolerance . . . losing performance focus Costs of mistakes
Corporate resource pool	Identified talent using common criteria across diverse businesses and functions Ensures developmental moves in corporate interest Provides mechanisms for tracking development over time and across boundaries Discovery and development of talent not dependent on individual bosses	Creates elitism—what happens to good people not knighted? Aggravates individual managers who lose control over their best people Propensity to develop overly elegant, lockstep, cookie cutter systems Danger of moving people too fast, too broadly, so they end up with breadth but no depth

Figure 6–2. (*Continued*)

Achieving this is no small accomplishment, and even then there are costs associated with the achievement. As figure 6–2 shows, a serious commitment to executive development may not be the right thing at the right time for every organization. Even if it is the "right" thing, these conditions may be difficult or impossible to achieve in a given organization. But development occurs to some degree in even the most hostile environments, so the issue is one of channeling, controlling, and enhancing whatever positive is already happening. This means *doing* things, and the remainder of this chapter is devoted to exploring what some of the options are for handling core issues in a developmental program. We will take a look at:

- identifying developmental jobs
- creating a talent pool
- dealing with breadth versus depth
- responsibility for the development process
- helping people learn from experience
- the role of coursework and training

Our purpose is to provide some concrete ideas for creating, implementing, and improving various components of an overall executive development program. The ideas were drawn largely from our own experiences with corporations working on executive succession and development programs, but are consistent with our research findings and with other research results.[5] But "how to" ideas are presented with the proviso that we know of no single "best way" for all organizations or for all high-potential managers in a given organization.

Identifying Developmental Jobs

Identifying developmental jobs is largely what this book has been about, especially chapter 2. We won't repeat the details here, but we will suggest that there are four basic processes that need to be accomplished: identifying developmental jobs that already exist, creating developmental experiences as appropriate, evaluating the chosen jobs, and keeping in touch with changes over time.

Identification can take several forms. One is to take for granted the results of our study and search the organization for start-ups, turn-arounds, projects, staff jobs, big-scope jobs, and good and bad bosses that meet the criteria. As we pointed out earlier, some kinds of experience are hidden away in unlikely places (for example, in international assignments or in small parts of the corporation) and need to be rooted out. Knowledgeable human resource people and line executives, in small groups or individually, can usually identify large numbers of relevant jobs in a short period of time.

A second approach is to repeat the form but not necessarily the substance of this research. By asking successful executives and other appropriate sources about the critical job experiences needed in the organization, you can produce a tailored list of developmental jobs. The key in this approach is to guide the respondents to look past job titles and "exposure" (a first instinct) and deal with managerial demands (see the "core elements" listed in chapter 5).

An assessment of what already exists is likely to reveal certain kinds of experiences that are rare or need to be beefed up. Some companies rarely use meaningful project assignments, for example, while others use them extensively. Some companies at this point in their history have few if any start-ups or maybe a shortage of big-scope jobs. Thus a second task is to create or beef up assignments to fill the "experience gaps" for high-potential managers. Some strategies for doing this were discussed earlier in this chapter.

The third component is evaluating the jobs identified as key to development. What kinds of challenges do they present? What lessons do they teach? How much risk to the organization does using them for development involve? This kind of information is crucial when actual placement decisions must be made.

Finally, it's absolutely essential to build in some level of mechanism for reassessing these key jobs regularly over the years. A change in boss or staff or business conditions could turn a potent experience into a mundane one, or vice versa. Certainly any job should be reconsidered before a developmental placement decision is made, suggesting the need for two basic systems: one that lays out the broad array of jobs tagged for executive development that can be used for career planning and organizational assessment purposes, and another that kicks in to reevaluate whenever a key manager is actually moved.

All this done, there remain two sticky issues. One is control over these crucial developmental jobs, which may mean creating a "corporate property" system for certain jobs as well as people. Related to that is the second issue, keeping these key jobs open for developmental use. Especially when a key job is held by a solid but plateaued performer, "unblocking" it can be a very serious issue.[6] In this case having a strong developmental ethic for all managers, not just the high potentials, might provide viable and acceptable moves for incumbents as well. Figure 6–3 presents a checklist for identifying developmental jobs.

Creating a Talent Pool

Earlier in this chapter we described some general principles for defining a pool of high-potential talent. Digging deeply, looking

---

☐ Identify existing types of jobs across corporation
- start-ups
- turn-arounds   or   • tailored list
- projects/task forces   for the
- scope   organization
- staff

☐ Create or enrich under-represented kinds of experiences

☐ Evaluate key developmental assignments
- challenges they present
- lessons to be learned
- risk to organization

☐ Mechanisms for constant updating, especially quick-reaction systems for placement decisions

☐ Decisions about control over key jobs

☐ Mechanism for unblocking key jobs

Figure 6–3. *Checklist for Identifying Developmental Jobs*

widely, applying common criteria, reassessing frequently, and using a corporate perspective are more easily espoused than done. When it comes to the nuts and bolts, once again there seem to be few definitive rules. The problem begins with the absence of common criteria for assessing leadership potential. While virtually every conceivable characteristic of leaders and managers has been studied at one time or another, the results of these efforts leave much to the imagination.[7] As yet, systematic research has not produced a list of ten or twenty or a hundred factors consistently and strongly related to effective executive leadership. (In fact, there is considerable disagreement about what effective leadership is, much less what "causes" it.) What agreement there is among scholars coalesces around the situational nature of leadership, suggesting that different qualities and abilities are required in different situations. This is no surprise to managers and executives, but it's no solution either. It explains, perhaps, why talent pools developed locally (for example, within business units or functional segments) may differ so dramatically from one another, but that only underlines the need to apply a broader perspective to the identification of high-potential talent for executive positions.

But even in the absence of convincing data on leadership attributes, *something* needs to be done. There are two basic tasks involved here, developing the criteria to be applied and developing the method of applying them. If identifying high potential is a judgment call, then who makes the judgment is a critical issue. The individual supervisor, embedded in a local context and focused on "getting the job done," is in a difficult position to make objective judgments of an individual's leadership potential several years down the road in a totally different context. Logically, then, some other mechanism would be helpful.

Perhaps the most elaborate technique for assessing future potential at lower and middle management levels is the assessment center method. Using standardized exercises, common criteria, and multiple raters (often high-level executives), assessment centers can be used across diverse businesses and functions and have a fairly consistent track record in predicting future success.[8] The tremendous expense of assessment centers has led some companies to develop standardized test batteries, which in some cases have proven equally valid.[9]

By far the most common method, however, in companies that do not rely on single-supervisor ratings, is committee review.[10] Small groups of managers or executives, usually assisted by their human resource staffs, assess the potential of managers in the units below them. Typically these committees convene at strategic levels of the hierarchy, with the results passed upward for final review at the highest levels. This exercise consumes a lot of time but can generate both a short-term succession plan and a longer term developmental plan for the key jobs in the business. It's not uncommon for companies that are serious about this process to generate upwards of two hundred high-potential managers for review at the management committee level. Fairly standard practice in such companies is to repeat the process annually and (usually through the human resource function) to monitor closely the progress and developmental plans of the individuals in the pool.

The issue of criteria to apply remains a nagging one, even when elaborate methods are used. Even a committee of executives only has data on an individual's performance in a given situation, and we've already discussed the fact that such information may not be predictive of performance in a different setting. In fact, track records of success may *not* distinguish executives who later succeed versus those who later derail.[11] While researchers continue their quest for a finite and generally applicable set of criteria for executive ability, we'd like to suggest that the lessons of experience described in this book provide a reasonable starting point. Described in detail in the earlier chapters, these clusters of skills and abilities include:

- the ability to set a reasonable agenda, reflecting perspective somewhat broader than the immediate job (for example, thinking one level up);
- the ability to handle diverse relationships, including different kinds of bosses, subordinates, customers, specialists, and so on;

- the temperament to adjust to givens of managerial life such as ambiguity, pressure, stress, and mistakes;
- demonstrated values consistent with the corporation's expectations of managerial integrity and the treatment of others;
- evidence of self-insight, reflected in the individual's awareness of his or her strengths and weaknesses and in the ability to learn from experience.

There may be some value, in addition to assessing virtues, in examining each individual's potential for derailment. The ten factors listed in figure 6–4 were described as reasons why talented people derailed later in their careers and might be detected early.

We believe the key to using these or other criteria[12] effectively lies in considering them in context. An individual can demonstrate an ability only when the job demands it. The ability to come up with a workable and strategic agenda is only tested when a manager has sufficient scope of responsibility and the latitude to establish a direction. One's values aren't demonstrated until one faces a dilemma that forces action either consistent or inconsistent with a value. The ability to cope with ambiguity is difficult to assess in an unambiguous job; how one will handle a mistake is hard to know until a mistake is made. We are suggesting that assessment of potential must be grounded in the demands of the specific jobs and assignments that individuals hold over time: keeping track of experience, if you will.

As we did the research, it became obvious that career histories in personnel files were less than useful in this regard. Even the most detailed records we ran across listed little more than job titles and dates of tenure. Looking over a twenty-year career history, containing as many as ten or fifteen jobs, it was impossible to tell what a manager had faced, much less what he or she had learned, from all that experience. At a minimum, corporate records on high-potential people should include the major demands faced in each assignment. Ideally, the records would also contain an assessment of how well a manager handled those core demands and how they developed. In a sense, the assignments one tackles are a living assessment center. Annual appraisals, usually focused on outcomes, say little about what was learned and even less about accumulation of learning over a career.

While our emphasis is development, it should be clear that identification of a high-potential pool is a *selection* issue. So is the choice of an individual for a specific assignment. This means that a viable executive development system must be fully coordinated with executive succession planning and decisions. Too often we see succession and development ensconced in totally different places in the organization and operated independently. More useful, we believe, are succession plans that deal specifically with developmental needs (as well as "ready now") and in which placement decisions are based on developmental strategies as well as business needs. Unless succession and development are intimately linked, we believe that selection, not development, will control executive resources.

Finally, elitism appears to be an almost inevitable effect of having a fast track (whether in school or in corporations), and it must be dealt with. Not being part of the elite group can have effects on the morale and motivation of solid performers. The anointed in turn may get the better jobs, more attention, higher salaries, and the like. A highly qualified solid manager may, for example, get passed over for a promotion so that a less experienced hotshot can have a developmental opportunity. As a counter to such effects, many corporations keep their high-potential lists secret, even from the high potentials. How much good this does is hard to say, since astute observers of their scene can probably figure it out. At worst, high potentials who don't know they are may perceive as a demotion or derailment a reassignment based on "secret" developmental intentions. As is true of salary information, there is controversy around secrecy in "hi-po" lists. Madness or not, we tend to side with candor. Minimally, individuals with potential should know why they are seen that way, what is expected of them, and why certain moves are seen as useful for them.

Fallout from fast track programs may be unavoidable, but one way of dealing with it is to have strong developmental programs for all employees (or at least managers). The hi-pos consti-

1. Specific performance problems with the business

   A series of performance problems sometimes emerges in which a manager runs into profit problems, gets lazy, or demonstrates that he can't handle certain kinds of jobs (usually new ventures or jobs requiring lots of persuasion). More important, by failing to admit the problem, covering it up, and trying to blame it on others, the manager shows that he can't change.

2. Insensitivity to others: an abrasive, intimidating, bullying style

   The most frequent cause for derailment was insensitivity to others. This often shows when managers are under stress.

3. Cold, aloof, arrogant

   Some managers are so brilliant that they become arrogant, intimidating others with their knowledge. Descriptive of such managers is this remark: "He made others feel stupid . . . wouldn't listen, had all the answers, wouldn't give you the time of day unless you were brilliant too."

4. Overly Ambitious: thinking of the next job, playing politics

   Some, like Cassius, are overly ambitious. They always seem to be thinking of their next job, bruising people in their haste, and spending too much time trying to please upper management.

5. Failing to staff effectively

   Some managers get along with their staff but simply pick the wrong people—staffing in their own image with technical specialists, or picking people who later fail.

6. Inability to think strategically

   Preoccupation with detail and a miring in technical problems keep some executives from grasping the bigger picture. They simply can't go from being doers to being planners.

7. Unable to adapt to a boss with a different style

   Failure to adapt appears as a conflict of style with a new boss. Although successful managers have the same problem, they don't get into wars over it, fight problems with facts, and rarely let the issues get personal.

4. Betrayal of trust

In an incredibly complex and confusing job, being able to trust others absolutely is a necessity. Some managers commit what is perhaps management's only unforgivable sin—they betray a trust. This rarely has anything to do with honesty (which was a given in almost all the cases); rather it is a one-upping of others or a failure to follow through on promises, which wreak havoc on organizational efficiency.

5. Overmanaging: failing to delegate or build a team

After a certain point, managers cease to do the work themselves and become executives who see that it is done. Some never make this transition, never learning to delegate or build a team beneath them. Although overmanaging is irritating at any level, at the executive level it can be fatal because of the difference in one's subordinates.

10. Overdependence on a mentor or advocate

Sometimes managers stay with a single advocate or mentor too long. When the mentor falls from favor, so do they. Even if the mentor remains in power, people question the executive's ability to make independent judgments. Can he stand alone, or does he need a mentor for a crutch?

Adapted from M. W. McCall, Jr., and M. M. Lombardo, *Off the Track: Why and How Successful Executives Get Derailed*, Technical Report No. 21 (Greensboro, N.C.: Center for Creative Leadership, January 1983).

Figure 6–4. *The Ten Fatal Flaws*

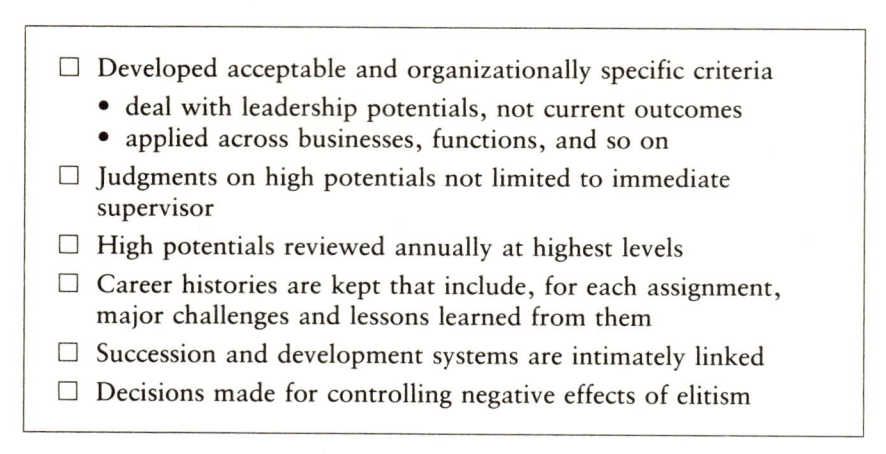

> ☐ Developed acceptable and organizationally specific criteria
>   - deal with leadership potentials, not current outcomes
>   - applied across businesses, functions, and so on
> ☐ Judgments on high potentials not limited to immediate supervisor
> ☐ High potentials reviewed annually at highest levels
> ☐ Career histories are kept that include, for each assignment, major challenges and lessons learned from them
> ☐ Succession and development systems are intimately linked
> ☐ Decisions made for controlling negative effects of elitism

Figure 6–5. *Checklist for Creating a Talent Pool*

tute a relatively small (albeit important) part of the managerial population. They are by no means the only ones who can grow and develop. One way to open blocked positions and enhance skills is to provide exciting opportunities for solid managers as well. Figure 6–5 presents a checklist for creating a talent pool.

Breadth versus Depth

Even the most contentious management committee will agree on the principle that their managers need more breadth, more exposure to other parts of the business, and broader perspective. But beneath that consensus lies adamant dissent. On corporate staff, achieving breadth may mean crossing businesses but staying in the same function. For line executives it may mean short stints in various functions or departments, such as operations or marketing, but within a single business. When the discussion gets to line managers crossing business segments, or requiring staff managers to have line experience, the temperature may go up. Perhaps in appeasement, the result is sometimes rotational systems for younger managers, hoping that "broad" exposure will have some lasting effects.

Making It Work

Breadth at the top is a critical issue, one we believe is not handled well through brief rotational assignments or willy-nilly transfers of more senior executives. Instead it must be approached as a serious part of the business strategy. Given where a company hopes to go, what kinds of experiences will best prepare future executives to operate in that environment? If crossing business segments is necessary to get certain experience, then the issue is settled. If certain staff functions really need to know specific things about operations, then the issue is how and where they can learn it. Sometimes the particular strengths of several businesses need to be combined for a future strategy.

The point is, there ought to be a *reason* for radical moves and shifts, and that reason should be connected to where the business is headed. It *is* possible to have too much breadth—to move so often that an individual develops truly superficial knowledge of almost everything. More often, however, managers reach the top with myopia built through long tenure in a single business or function. The answer to "How much breadth is enough?" is "How much breadth do you need?" Restated, the issue for an individual's development is "What might be learned from that experience that will enhance an executive's ability to achieve the strategy?" Careers are not long enough for a top executive to have hands-on experience with every major part of a corporate giant. So we come full circle. An organization that can't figure out where it's headed will have a devil of a time developing the talent to get it there. (See figure 6–6.)

☐ Differing meanings for "breadth" (for example, line versus staff)

☐ Business strategy implications for developmental cross-boundary movement are clearly spelled out

☐ Individual knows the reason for a specific cross-boundary move

---

Figure 6–6. *Checklist for Breadth versus Depth Issues*

Responsibility for the Development Process

> It's *my* job to develop my people, not some staff group's. Human resource people can be a cop-out—some managers use them to avoid their own responsibilities.
> —A senior line executive

The deficit. The value of the dollar. International competition. The balance of trade. Vulnerability to hostile takeover. Poor product quality. The list of major issues needing senior management attention is indeed an impressive one. Taxes, interest rates, raw materials and labor costs, market share, new technology, obsolescence . . . on and on. It's easy to say development is a line responsibility, but how realistic is it to expect management development to get the attention it requires from line executives? The answer, we believe, is "not very." The corporations we've worked with that do a good job of development frequently have a strong, talented human resource staff that works well with the line. They vary in how the function is organized—decentralized versus centralized, emphasis on selection versus development, numbers and titles, and the like—but not much in the function's influence and competence.

It's always risky to give prescriptions, but our experience as well as inferences drawn from executives' descriptions of their own development strongly suggest some parameters. First, control of managerial and executive development *has to* reside in line and functional managers, and specifically in the top management group.[13] Only they can set and hold to the priority and shape a culture supportive of growth.

Second, even with a clear priority and significant time devoted to development, the human resource staff has a critical role. It was best described by members of the management committee in a company we recently studied, who described what they wanted from the human resource staff. Boiled down, they wanted their human resource people to:

- provide solid data to use in making developmental decisions and plans;

- act as their conscience, to assure that it was done, and done well;
- be a source of ideas on how to do it better;
- persuade, cajole, nudge, and nag: in short, to make it happen; and,
- help in articulating the vision and developing the strategy for a solid developmental system in the organization.

Perhaps the best analogy is the role that financial staff serve in an effective organization. They act as partners, applying their expertise in consort with the line decision makers.

This approach has a number of implications, beginning with the "qualifications" desirable in a human resource staff. The traditional credentials in the specialty area of human resources are part of the picture, but the harder part lies in that elusive quality, credibility. To work as a partner, persuader, of senior management requires credibility, as so many of the executives we interviewed had learned the hard way. What is credibility for a human resource person if not simply functional expertise? It's knowing the business and knowing the people. How else can a staff person recommend certain assignments for their developmental potential? How else can a staff person participate in an assessment of a high-potential manager? The executives we studied emphasized hands-on learning and the necessity for knowing the business. It's no different for a staff person charged with the development of management talent. It is not a theoretical or abstract proposition. Maybe that's why in many developmentally oriented companies we find human resource staff with some line experience, reporting to line managers (with dotted lines to corporate staff) and dispersed across the businesses.

It doesn't stop there, though. Senior management bears responsibility for empowering qualified human resource professionals. In addition to setting the priority and committing their time to development, senior management needs to put teeth into their commitment. (See figure 6–7.) This takes many forms in the corporate world, but we have seen the following:

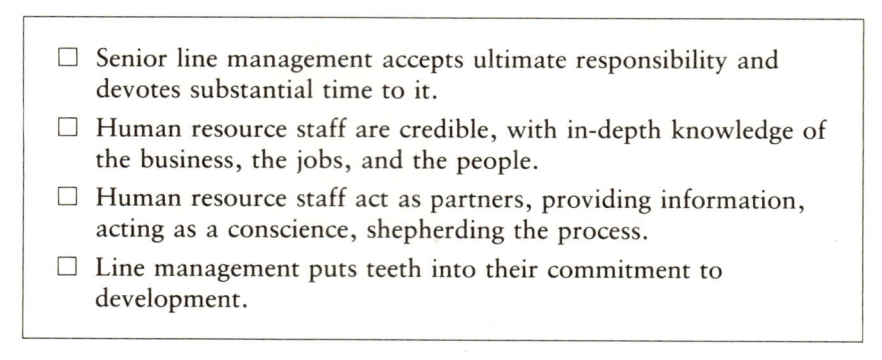

> ☐ Senior line management accepts ultimate responsibility and devotes substantial time to it.
> ☐ Human resource staff are credible, with in-depth knowledge of the business, the jobs, and the people.
> ☐ Human resource staff act as partners, providing information, acting as a conscience, shepherding the process.
> ☐ Line management puts teeth into their commitment to development.

Figure 6-7. *Checklist for Responsibility for Development*

- 25 percent of executives' bonuses tied directly to achieving developmental objectives
- the position of Senior Executive Vice President of Human Resources, who sits on the management committee
- routine participation by human resource staff in management meetings on succession and placement

Helping People Learn from Experience

Even though the final responsibility for learning must lie with the individual (see chapter 5), there are many things the organization can do—both directly and indirectly—to help people learn. The list is no doubt a long one, and we can touch on only a few ideas here. They include the critical first management job, issues around timing, help with critical transitions, making corrections, and finally, the roles that immediate superiors can play.

Help with the First Management Job. For many of the executives we studied, their first management job was still a potent memory as long as twenty-five years later. The challenge in this job was in leading others for the first time, and many future executives came to the simple yet basic realization that management decisions were made on a different basis than technical decisions. As one well-seasoned executive put it:

> I've seen young people we've had to let go because they never learned that management is different from technical work. They arrived at the best technical decisions and that's that. They don't try to persuade others and they're insensitive to others' needs.
>
> We put in a drilling rig in China recently and the Chinese, beyond their technical staff, wanted to have seventy-three observers. Now there's not much room on those rigs, but that's the way the Chinese like to learn. The young man who was in charge said sure, that's fine, but lots of others I've seen wouldn't have and everyone would have come out the loser.

His point is a critical one, which addresses the basic psychological transition from professional to manager. Unless this lesson is learned quickly, young managers are likely to derail later. Learning from this early exposure to management is something many organizations leave up to chance, but it is a career turning point where young people often need help. No executive mentioned a supervision course as having been important in this learning process, but *most* credited a boss who took the time to help them.

While we will address bosses specifically later, the crucial observation is that this change from specialist to manager is so important that it may deserve special attention in an executive development program. The choice of the assignment, the boss that goes with it, and special interventions can have dramatic effects on a fledgling high-potential manager.

Help through the Timing of Events. One of the indirect ways of influencing development is by timing interventions and job changes carefully. By this we mean active consideration of particular assignments in the careers of high-potential managers and what can be done to maximize learning. For example, young high-potential managers usually log significant hours in the core of the business. This presents some challenges to learning, because the depth of experience can limit the breadth. Projects, line-to-staff switches, and small scopes are excellent vehicles for exposure to other units and challenges without leaving the core prematurely.

Any career also goes through slack periods, where new major challenges are not available. Here we recommend fillers with power—perhaps a special project assignment in addition to the present job.

How long a person should stay in a job is a subject of much debate and myth in organizations. At one extreme, people sometimes are kept in jobs well past any developmental payoff; at the other, people sometimes are moved from some important jobs before development is realized. A major assignment (such as the big fix-its and scopes we described in chapter 2) takes roughly three years to master because on-line learning follows several distinct stages. As Gabarro has shown, managers first act on the most familiar problems (that is, marketing people work on marketing issues), only later immersing themselves in learning the other aspects of the job.[14] This is followed by a second wave of activity as problems that were not initially obvious came to the fore. Finally came the consolidation and refinement phases. We have spoken with many executives who were intuitively aware of this. "Just when I figured out what the critical problems were, I was transferred," one said. Another commented that "I've always had time to fix it but never enough to fix it right."

In some companies, the rate of growth is such that managers believe, "Move in eighteen months or you're off the fast track." Moving people quickly may be a necessity, but it extracts a significant developmental cost. The cases Gabarro studied involved a reshaping period when the job lasted more than eighteen months, and managers learned at a deeper level after this point than they did during the initial wave.

In summary, many young managers never really get to finish a job, much less consolidate and refine what they have learned from it. Careful consideration of completing the job, not simply doing a short stint in it, is necessary for meaningful development to occur.

Help with Critical Transitions. Obviously, the first managerial assignment (discussed earlier) is a critical transition of major importance. But there are at least two other kinds of management transitions that organizations can help managers with: increases in complexity and increases in scope and scale. Managers who must learn to cope with great complexity can be helped by moving them through jobs that gradually increase demands. One progression, for example, might be from managing a new group to managing a new product rollout with a new group to creating a new business.

Increases in the scope and scale of responsibility (discussed in the "scope" section of chapter 2) are commonly associated with becoming a general manager. The work of Kotter and Gabarro can be useful here in helping managers learn to ask the right questions, assist others in figuring out what to do for themselves, spot danger signs, and learn on the run more efficiently.[15]

Because many significant management jobs contain increases in complexity and scale, help with these issues needs to begin with young managers. Once again, executive development begins long before a person reaches executive rank.

Making Corrections. Mistakes and failures are as inevitable in a career as the blind spots and flaws that contribute to them. Yet hardship or derailment counseling is something many organizations are loath to do, sometimes because the matters are personal, or sometimes because it's easier to believe such action is unnecessary, that bright people will figure things out for themselves.

Bright people often don't. As we argued in chapters 4 and 5, learning from setbacks can be the most difficult learning of all. Sensitive counseling can be necessary for the most stable of individuals, and special assignments and even "penalty boxes," coupled with straight feedback, may save a career.

In other words, people may need some help in getting the message about their flaws and mistakes. The larger the record of success and positive feedback, the more likely it is that such help will be needed, and the more dramatic the message may have to be. But if the goal is to help a person take responsibility for self-development, then helping him or her see that there is a problem is a fundamental prerequisite.

The Role of the Boss. The discussion so far makes it clear that the immediate supervisor can play a pivotal role in the development of executive talent. Particularly because the individual who needs development may not be able to see himself or herself objectively, or may not be able to exert control over events, the immediate boss can become the second most central player in individual development.

In chapter 3 we discussed at length how bosses influenced learning, for better or for worse. In chapter 2 we reviewed the critical role bosses sometimes played in the learning from important assignments (especially in big-scope changes). Bosses even played important roles in some of the hardships (chapter 4), especially in how they handled their subordinates' mistakes and in the feedback they gave after missed promotions, exiles, and demotions.

What we saw in those chapters was amazing variety in the kinds of roles bosses might play. They could:

- leave a person alone, allowing him or her to take responsibility;
- assure that an individual was constantly challenged in the job;
- provide help by giving advice, suggestions, feedback, and coaching;
- allow an individual to observe the inner workings of an activity (particularly in an area of the boss's real talent) by inviting him or her into the action;
- buffer the individual from the system, allowing him or her room to make mistakes;
- play the heavy, getting a person's attention through reprimand, punishment, warning; and
- alternate tough and supportive action, as called for.

Unfortunately, not all bosses are well suited for all of those roles (indeed, the boss may not be as talented as the high-potential manager!), nor are such activities necessarily top priority for someone who has a business to run. Some organizations attempt to force their managers into developmental roles through performance appraisal systems, training them in feedback and coaching skills, morale surveys that measure developmental efforts, and even attaching some part of compensation to efforts at development. These procedures are built on the assumption that even if all managers aren't equally adept at developing others, all managers can do a better job of it. There is some merit to the argument, but the heart of the matter remains in a very personal relationship between a specific boss and a specific subordinate. As we noted earlier, terrible bosses can have positive developmental impact, and sometimes just having the boss geographically far away was a positive developmental move.

This brings us back to an earlier point. With the possible exception of the need for a really good boss in a few specific assignments, it appears that *variety* in kinds of bosses over a career is what matters developmentally. Because a boss/subordinate relationship is a personal one, mentoring cannot be forced. Nor is it necessarily a good idea to put responsibility for development solely on the boss's shoulders even if it could be done.

This leaves us with two ways to view the managers of high-potential individuals. On the one hand, bosses are a direct part of experience, and those who work for them take away lessons based on the relationship. The behavior of superiors is a potent force in the shaping of values for developing managers, and the particular talents of particular bosses sometimes rub off on subordinates.

The other view is that bosses are a potent developmental tool which the organization can use as part of its broader strategy for developing executive resources. By viewing managers as part of the developmental process, the organization can influence the context in which individual growth takes place. While the growth of an individual is necessarily idiosyncratic, the organization has significant influence, over time and across people. Just as personal growth involves choices for the individual, en-

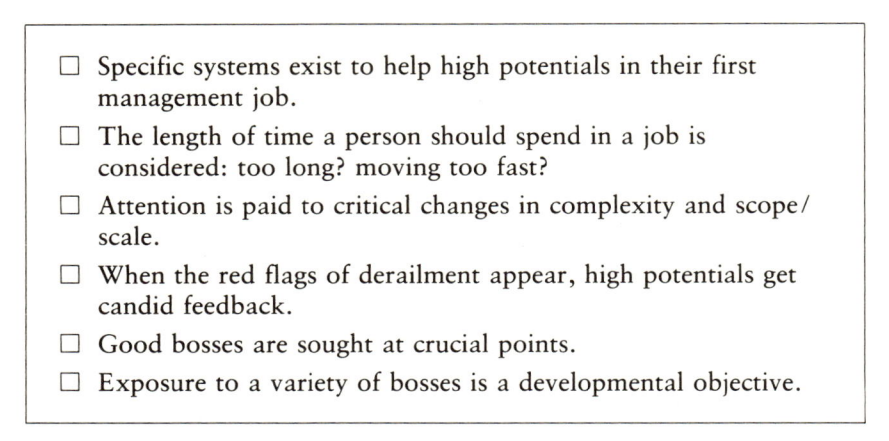

> ☐ Specific systems exist to help high potentials in their first management job.
> ☐ The length of time a person should spend in a job is considered: too long? moving too fast?
> ☐ Attention is paid to critical changes in complexity and scope/scale.
> ☐ When the red flags of derailment appear, high potentials get candid feedback.
> ☐ Good bosses are sought at crucial points.
> ☐ Exposure to a variety of bosses is a developmental objective.

Figure 6–8. *Checklist for Helping People Learn from Experience*

suring the development of adequate numbers of capable executives, and exposing them to talented bosses, involves choices for the organization. Figure 6–8 presents a checklist for helping people learn from experience.

Helping through Coursework. Our intent in this book has been to focus on development on the job, where most of it occurs. Formal coursework, however, was sometimes included by executives as an event that made a significant difference to them.[16] But the courses that made a big difference usually weren't routine. They weren't in the normal, straight-through educational process (undergraduate and graduate work done contiguously) and rarely were limited to specific technical areas. The courses that mattered were usually attended voluntarily, occurred later in one's career, and dealt with general management and business issues or process/self-analysis. Over half occurred in university settings (such as advanced management programs at Harvard, Dartmouth, MIT, and Wharton), and almost all were conducted away from the job. Coursework that had an impact on the executives seemed to have two things in common: it dealt with a relevant issue, and it occurred at a good time for the manager.

Ironically, the major outcome was not usually the content of the course but the confidence engendered by the experience. This took several forms:

- confidence in career progress resulting from being chosen for a plum—an exclusive or high-prestige course (for example, Harvard, Sloan, and so on)
- confidence from discovering that one knew more about some area than one had thought (for example, a manager who learned finance on the job and discovered that he or she already knew what the course covered)
- confidence from discovering that the manager was as capable as managers from other well-known firms who also attended the course

The content itself made the biggest difference when the manager needed it at once back on the job. For example, one manager took a course in organizational design while assigned to a task force to redesign the corporation. Another attended a workshop on stress during a particularly rough time.

Coursework can also expose managers to different ways of thinking about problems, not in a textbook sense but through working with other people with different problem-solving approaches. "It was fascinating to learn how a marketing or finance guy approached issues," one said.

Finally, reexamining one's view of the balance between life and work (the "who am I" and "what do I really want" questions) sometimes resulted from a classroom experience. When a course included careful self-examination and candid feedback, it sometimes helped managers face such potentially derailing flaws as arrogance or insensitivity or a proclivity to go it alone. The time away, coupled with the stimulation and reflection that coursework can offer, seems to be one of the few safe, reliable ways to help managers with these important questions.

In a sense, timing and colleagues are everything in coursework. This does not mean that other kinds of courses have no value, but it does suggest that some common practices may have less impact for high-potential managers. Among them:

- lockstep course sequences for all managers at a given stage (for example, the entire middle management group)
- courses with no prestige factor (highly heterogeneous mixes of talent and success among participants)
- courses whose content has little connection with the work the manager is doing (for example, content unrelated to the job, or general models that hold little specific utility)
- courses whose instructors lack credibility—whose experience or capability is inferior to that of the manager
- remedial or forced courses, where a manager has to attend against his or her own desires or needs

Like other experiences that made a difference, high-impact courses had an element of a test. Am I as good as executives from a renowned company? Do I know as much about (marketing or finance or global competition) as the experts? Can I handle the intellectual demands of a Harvard? Can I deal with a full-time job, school, and family all at the same time?

Of course, as executives ascend and their responsibilities grow, finding time and inclination to invest in courses becomes more difficult. One strategy for training at higher levels is to couple such experiences with staff or project assignments where a manager is more likely to focus on a task for which course content would be useful. Another strategy is to design courses to coincide with difficult transitions—for example, taking charge of a general manager job for the first time.

At their best, courses provide insight into strengths and areas in which a manager might improve or try new things. They do not substitute for on-the-job learning and should not be asked to serve that purpose. (See figure 6–9.) Properly used, coursework enhances careers, but it is not a cure-all for every conceivable personal deficit.

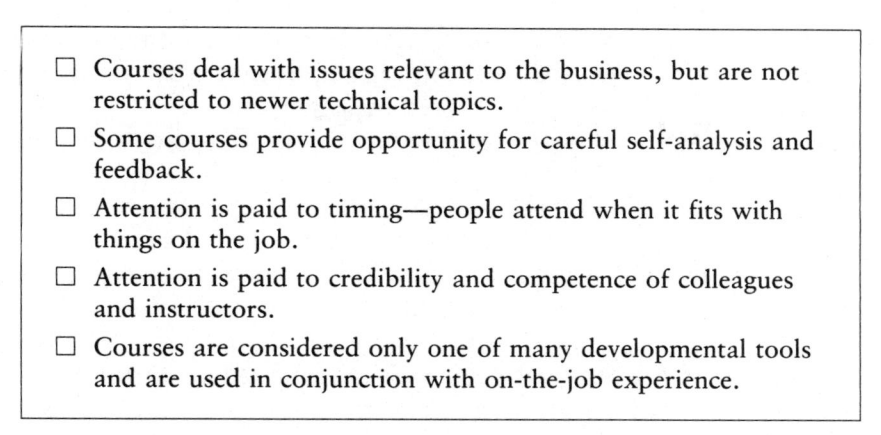

> - ☐ Courses deal with issues relevant to the business, but are not restricted to newer technical topics.
> - ☐ Some courses provide opportunity for careful self-analysis and feedback.
> - ☐ Attention is paid to timing—people attend when it fits with things on the job.
> - ☐ Attention is paid to credibility and competence of colleagues and instructors.
> - ☐ Courses are considered only one of many developmental tools and are used in conjunction with on-the-job experience.

Figure 6–9. *Checklist for Coursework and Training*

A Scorecard for Executive Development Systems

To be sure, most of the well-managed companies bristle with formal human resource systems. Succession plans, performance appraisals, training catalogs, career pathing manuals, policy books, assessment centers, and special programs abound. This degree of formality may contribute to human resource development (especially in institutionalizing it), but we don't believe the measure of effective practice is the number of policy manuals and forms. More important is the *way* it's done—the characteristics of the process that implements the commitment we have already described. Development is not magic. It is not a science. It does not lend itself to neat formulas, precise measures of this and that.

Coping with variety and adversity seems to be our lot. This is where the lessons of experience take hold. How they take hold, how one develops, is much harder to specify, but more often than not we seem to grow when our lives are not programmable. We seem to develop best when caught up in that curious mixture of attraction and fear we call excitement. Too often we forget that and try to design the perfect system to punch out top executives routinely. We would happily make the same mistake Lewis Thomas describes for biologists if they had designed DNA: "Our molecule would have been perfect. . . . [I]t would never have occurred to us, thinking as we do, that the thing had to be able to make errors."[17]

People have to do it themselves, this developmental business. The role of a "system" is to help people do that, and we conclude that an effective system for developing executive resources would have the following characteristics:

1. Opportunistic. Some of America's best-managed corporations are tenacious when it comes to moving their high-potential managers through developmental assignments. But even in the best, the business comes first. It's folly to put a rookie in an assignment that could sink the company—at least not if there's a choice. So business risk will outweigh development a lot of the time. Certainly the critical experiences described to us were frequently driven by fortune. Often there was no choice—you're it. Bosses died or quit or left. Business got so fouled up that a rookie was sent to see if he or she could do better than the pros. Right time, right place happened all the time.

Sometimes assignments were chosen deliberately as testing grounds, and so sometimes were some of the bosses people were assigned to. But there was little control over divorces, the chaos of mergers, when mistakes were made, demonstrations of values, and the like. Some of the most potent experiences came from pure chance. So the basic rule is, don't expect developmental goals to control the career experiences of a talented executive. People who like lockstep systems treat serendipity as an enemy and are doomed to frustration.

So if they can't control it, effective human resource systems make the most of it. They take advantage of serendipitous events, creating more of them (more choices), being ready to respond to them. Because you can control only some of what happens, you've got to be ready to go with what happens. Scrambling is the starting point, not an afterthought, in designing executive development systems.

In executive development, the ability to scramble means

knowing what kinds of experiences are potentially developmental for what,[18] and being able at a moment's notice to tweak or nudge or leverage opportunities when they appear. Opportunism means getting out there, seeing the jobs, knowing the people, knowing the bosses, getting a feel for the demands.

So the first measure of an opportunistic system is a human resource staff who know what jobs have what developmental potential, who are close enough to the jobs and the business to nudge and persuade at the crucial moment, and who can show how a developmental decision is also a solid business decision. Charts and graphs and systems and theories won't cut it, only firsthand, solid, credible knowledge.

Opportunism is scrambling, making do, throwing out safety nets, finding options. Above all, it's making decisions that are better for the business. It's finding ways to add developmental potential to existing jobs, to find jobs that make similar demands even in a business that isn't starting new business from scratch. It's finding or creating big-scope jobs earlier in a career (overseas, for example). It's keeping an eye peeled for opportunities to let talented people grow.

Most line executives want to keep talented people challenged. They naturally think of assignments that may broaden the skills of their best. A nudge, the leverage, is in helping them do that with a little better precision. It's looking at the options that exist and helping determine who may grow the most. It's not optimal, it's not a grand strategic plan, but it makes the difference.

2. *Individualistic.* People are different; top executives are different. People grow and learn at different rates, in different ways, from different things. Executive development has to be individualistic, and an effective developmental system will treat it as such. Each person is a unique tapestry of strengths and weaknesses, and an effective system must know each person well enough to match developmental needs with developmental opportunity (and be consistent with business needs as well). Human resource staff and line managers must know the people. The most sophisticated information system is no substitute for

firsthand, direct knowledge, and an individualistic system will have ways of keeping the high potentials visible to important decision-makers.

3. Long Term. As John Kotter observed, executive development occurs over a lifetime.[19] A long-term perspective is essential in executive development. Diversity of experience can occur only over time, as does the learning that may come from it. The problem is that the *sequence* of experience has received more attention than it merits; diversity, balance, and change less attention than they deserve. Without growth and change, diversity per se means little. Exposure, over the years, to different kinds of assignments, bosses, demands. Assessment, over time, of development resulting from exposure to specific demands. Balance, over time, between short-duration, focused projects, and longer term, full-responsibility jobs, between team efforts and solo flights.

So yet another indicator of an effective system is its focus on ten–twenty years for development rather than on crash courses.

4. Self-motivated. Development is not something you do *to* someone or *for* someone. Primary responsibility for learning, growth, and change resides in the manager, not in the boss, development committee, or human resource specialist. Their responsibility lies in providing learning opportunities, help at crucial points, and hard-nosed assessment. Effective developmental systems create conditions in which people can do it for themselves.

Here are some basic principles that might guide a system that motivates people to develop themselves:

- Assignments are sought that create a desire to learn. The desire to learn is particularly high when new knowledge or skills are needed to do the job better. Desire to learn becomes a need to learn when success itself depends on mastery.
- Resources are provided to assist in learning. These might include access to experienced people, availability of specialized staff, adequate funding to retain outside specialists, and so

forth. A manager in high action may not have time for a three-week marketing course at Harvard but may have two hours on a Sunday morning to spend being tutored by an expert.

- It has the teeth to bring a high-potential manager up short when necessary. Effective managers tend to have a lot of confidence, even arrogance. Whatever weaknesses they have, they've managed to be successful anyway. It may take feedback in no uncertain terms to get their attention—maybe even a demotion.

- "For your own good" is explained. Many stories we heard, especially those involving lateral moves or apparent backward steps, were laced with anger. It was only later that the manager realized the move was intended as developmental rather than punitive. Much ill will could have been spared had the manager been told the purpose of the move and its duration.

- People who try and fail are protected. Even though almost everyone readily admits that learning requires risk and inevitable mistakes, tolerance of mistakes that affect the business is sometimes zero. A learning environment contains second chances, temporary penalty boxes, and a tone that suggests that some mistakes are tolerated as long as you learn from them.

- Some time for reflection and analysis is provided. The managerial world is action-oriented and filled with opportunities for learning. Success and pace together are dangerous to growth if not punctuated with some time to consolidate learning. The period immediately after a major challenging assignment may be the most crucial time of all to step back and assess what just happened. (And the hardest to pull off. Especially if successful, the hero will likely report to the next assignment on Monday.) We have advocated extreme measures—such as a "forced" vacation for a week at the remotest beach available—just to allow for reflection. Guided reflection, in the safety of a training setting, might be even more powerful. It is staggering to think how much experience is wasted simply because managers aren't allowed, or forced, to stop and make sense of what happened.

So an effective system will help people motivate themselves by stretching their ability, providing resources, getting their attention, being straightforward in what's happening, encouraging trial and error, and providing time for reflection.

5. On Line. By now, it should go without saying that we believe significant learning must occur on line. That is, it's dealing with *real* problems and facing *real* consequences. Whether we are talking about medical students, student pilots, or future executives, there comes a time when simulations and theory are replaced by the real thing.

The message to people charged with developing executive resources is straightforward. The challenge lies in making better use of on-the-job experiences. This means finding better ways to identify developmentally significant jobs, to move the right people to them, and to help talented people learn from them. How well these things are done is far more important than how formal or elegant the procedures are.

Appendix
The Original Interview Guide

Interview Format
Research Sponsor Program

Preparation for Section I

When you think about your career as a manager, certain events or episodes probably stand out in your mind—things that led to a *lasting change* in your approach to management. Please jot down some notes for yourself identifying at least three "key events" in your career: things that made a difference in the way you manage now. When we meet with you, we'll ask you about each event:

1. What happened?
2. What did you learn from it (for better or worse)?

Section II: Key Events

Having talked about key events that really stood out for you, we'll now address some things that may or may not have had a lasting effect on you. Because our time is limited, we need your help in controlling it. As you look over the questions, some are no doubt more meaningful to you than others. Please be prepared to go into some depth on the important ones, and comment briefly on the others. Still other questions may have been answered in the first section.

A. *Rites of Passage*

1. What was your first managerial job? Was there anything special about it? About your first boss?

2. What was your first "quantum leap"—movement to a job with significantly more responsibility/challenge/pressure than prior jobs?

3. What was your first important exposure to high-level executives? Have there been others that stand out for you?

4. What was your "organizational first date"—like your first real date, a time when you were all alone and had to take complete responsibility for something you'd never done before?

5. What was the biggest challenge you ever faced?

6. What was your most frightening first—something you did for the first time that really had you worried?

7. What event (or events) made you realize you were going to be successful as a manager? In this organization?

B. *Rising from the Ashes*

1. What was your darkest hour?

2. What was a significant near miss—a time when you tried something and failed?

3. Describe a time when you pushed things to the brink—that is, a time when you stretched the system by coming perilously close to violating rules, norms, or authority.

4. What was your most significant act of procrastination? By this we mean a time when you didn't face up to a situation that got steadily worse, resulting in a mess.

5. Do you recall a time when you had the rug pulled out from under you—a situation when you had everything ready to go and the door was slammed shut?

Appendix

6. Were you ever worn out or fed up, but managed to restart?
7. Did you ever learn a great truth that turned out to be a falsehood? That is, was there ever a case where you thought you'd learned something significant but later found out it wasn't so?
8. Was there a situation you took very seriously at the time but were able to laugh about months (or years) later?

C. *The Role of Other People*

1. Please describe the person who taught you the most during your career. What did that person do that made him or her so special?
2. Most of us have worked for a person we simply couldn't tolerate for one reason or another. What did you learn from such an experience?
3. What was your most significant interpersonal conflict—a situation in which dealing with another person (or persons) was very difficult for you?

Section III: General Questions

1. Overall, how have you changed, plus and minus, over your career? If you ran into someone who knew you well years ago, what differences would he or she notice?
2. Are there times when you've been more open to learning than others? More closed?
3. What part have events in your personal life played in your growth as a manager?
4. What about being a manager has been fun for you? What are some examples of situations or events you particularly enjoyed? That were the most fun?

5. What advice would you give to a younger manager about managing his or her career? What do you need to do for yourself? How much should you let others do for you (or to you)?
6. What is the most significant thing you've learned as an adult—the one thing you'd pass on to someone else if you could?
7. What's next? Are you facing a situation now from which you expect to learn something new?

Notes

Chapter 1. Developing Executive Talent

1. A. Short, "The Corporate Classroom: Are We Getting Our Money's Worth?" *New Management* 4 (Winter 1987):22–26; and J.P. Kotter, *The Leadership Factor* (New York: Free Press, 1988).
2. From a conversation with a senior human resource executive in a Fortune 500 corporation. The figure includes costs associated with selecting, relocating, supporting, outplacing, and replacing the failed executive, but not the business losses (which can be considerably more).
3. D.T. Hall, *Careers in Organizations* (Pacific Palisades, Calif.: Goodyear Publishing Company, 1976). Also D.W. Bray, R.J. Campbell, and D.L. Grant, *Formative Years in Business: A Long-Term AT&T Study of Managerial Lives* (New York: Wiley, 1974).
4. Kotter, *The Leadership Factor*.
5. C.D. McCauley, *Developmental Experiences in Managerial Work: A Literature Review,* Technical Report No. 26 (Greensboro, N.C.: Center for Creative Leadership, 1986), 2.
6. Tom Bouchard reportedly found, in his research on twins reared apart, that 61 percent of leadership was genetically determined. See "All About Twins," *Newsweek,* November 23, 1987, 69.
7. For an interesting discussion of inherent gifts and developed abilities among gifted people, see B.S. Bloom, "Generalizations About Talent Development," in *Developing Talent in Young People,* ed. B.S. Bloom (New York: Ballantine, 1985), 507–549.
8. J.P. Kotter, *The General Managers* (New York: Free Press, 1982).
9. For comprehensive reviews see B.M. Bass, ed., *Stogdill's Handbook of Leadership* (New York: Free Press, 1981) and J.P. Campbell, M.D. Dunnette, E.E. Lawler III, and K.E. Weick, Jr., *Managerial Behavior, Performance, and Effectiveness* (New York: McGraw–Hill, 1970).

10. R. Klimoski and M. Brickner, "Why Do Assessment Centers Work? The Puzzle of Assessment Center Validity," *Personnel Psychology* 40 (1987):243–260.
11. Kotter, *The General Managers.*
12. Kotter, *The Leadership Factor.*
13. For a discussion of how science works, see L. Thomas, *Late Night Thoughts on Listening to Mahler's Ninth Symphony* (New York: Viking, 1983), 18–28.
14. In the first study, 79 executives from three corporations were interviewed. Three additional studies used open-ended surveys to generate the same information from an additional 112 executives (samples of 28, 20, and 64) from three more corporations. The overall sample contained almost all white males, averaging in their early to mid forties.
15. The terms *successful* and *executive* are often bandied about but seldom defined. Neither term, we discovered, is easy to pin down. To identify successful executives, we worked closely with senior human resource and line management to generate hand-picked samples of people judged to have the best shot at the top jobs in each company. Thus *success* was defined in terms of each company studied, and included both success to date *and* judgments about future potential.

    Executive is not a term that means the same thing across organizations. To ensure that samples were roughly comparable across companies, we used position on the organization chart, salary grades, Hay points, or whatever data we could get that reflected responsibility and hierarchical level. Titles in our final sample ranged from high-level functional managers and directors or general managers through chief executive, and varied according to organization structure. Whether a person was technically an executive depended on how the particular organization defined the term (for example, top 150 jobs, bonus eligible, or a certain grade point level).
16. When the studies were done, five of the six corporations were American firms in the Fortune 50 industrials. The sixth firm was a major subsidiary of a comparably sized Canadian corporation.
17. A thorough, systematic analysis of these data is E. Lindsey, V. Homes, and M.W. McCall, Jr., *Key Events in Executives' Lives,* Technical Report No. 32 (Greensboro, N.C.: Center for Creative Leadership, 1987).
18. These themes were first described in Lindsey et al., *Key Events in Executives' Lives,* 225–228. This book also describes each of the lessons in great detail.
19. Kotter, *The General Managers.*
20. Ibid., 66.
21. The criteria used to decide which lessons are associated with each event (that is, the ones highlighted in the figures) and the data are reported in full in Lindsey et al., *Key Events in Executives' Lives.*
22. Kotter, *The Leadership Factor,* 81–82.
23. Also see M.M. Lombardo and M.W. McCall, Jr., "Great Truths That May Not Be," *Issues and Observations,* February 1983:1–4.

Chapter 2. Trial by Fire: Learning from Job Assignments

1. Quotations from executives used throughout the book are either direct quotes (from the open-ended surveys) or reconstructed from interview notes. Many have been altered slightly to protect anonymity or confidentiality.
2. M.W. McCall, Jr., and M.M. Lombardo, "What Makes a Top Executive?" *Psychology Today,* February 1983, 26–31. Also Hall, *Careers in Organizations.*
3. Bray, Campbell, and Grant, *Formative Years in Business.*
4. D.W. MacKinnon, "The Assessment and Development of Managerial Creativity," Invited address, Third International Congress on the Assessment Center Method, Quebec City, Quebec, Canada, May 28–30, 1975.
5. Kotter, *The Leadership Factor.*
6. G. Jennings, *The Mobile Manager* (New York: McGraw-Hill, 1971).
7. E. Schein, *Career Dynamics: Matching Individual and Organizational Needs* (Reading, Mass.: Addison–Wesley, 1978).
8. R.J. Grey and G.G. Gordon, "Risk-Taking Managers: Who Gets the Top Jobs," *Management Review* 67 (1978):8–13.
9. D.C. Hambrick, "Environment, Strategy and Power Within Top Management Teams," *Administrative Science Quarterly* 26 (1981):253–275.
10. McCauley, *Developmental Experiences in Managerial Work.*
11. W. Skinner and E. Sasser, *Manufacturing in the Corporate Strategy* (New York: Wiley, 1978).
12. F. Allen, "Bosses List Main Strengths, Flaws Determining Potential of Managers," *Wall Street Journal,* November 14, 1980.
13. Kotter, *The Leadership Factor.*
14. J. Sonnenfeld and J.P. Kotter, "The Maturation of Career Theory," *Human Relations* 35 (1982):29.
15. C. Margerison and A. Kakabadse, *How American Chief Executives Succeed* (New York: American Management Association, 1984).
16. W.F. Dowling, "Conversation: An Interview With Fletcher Byrom," *Organizational Dynamics* 7 (1978): 41.
17. Bass, *Stogdill's Handbook of Leadership,* 553–583.
18. Schein, *Career Dynamics.*
19. D.W. Bray and A. Howard, "Career Success and Life Satisfactions of Middle-Aged Managers," In *Competence and Coping During Adulthood,* ed. L.A. Bond and J.C. Rosen (Hanover, N.H.: University Press of New England, 1980), 22.
20. H. Mintzberg, *The Nature of Managerial Work* (New York: Harper and Row, 1973).
21. A review of these studies can be found in M.W. McCall, Jr., A.M. Morrison, and R.L. Hannan, *Studies of Managerial Work: Results and Methods,* Techni-

cal Report No. 9 (Greensboro, N.C.: Center for Creative Leadership, May 1978). Also see L. Sayles, *Leadership* (New York: McGraw–Hill, 1979), 1–24.
22. Kotter, *The General Managers,* 143.

Chapter 3. When Other People Matter

1. Cited by McCauley, *Developmental Experiences in Managerial Work,* 10.
2. Ibid., 12.
3. Marshall and Stewart, "Managers' Job Perceptions: Their Overall Frameworks and Working Strategies" (*Journal of Management Studies* 18:177–190) cited by McCauley, *Developmental Experiences in Managerial Work,* 12.
4. Clawson, "Mentoring in Managerial Careers" (In C.B. Derr, ed., *Work, Family, and the Career*), cited by McCauley, *Developmental Experiences in Managerial Work,* 10.
5. In addition to interviewing the executive, we were able to talk with four of his former subordinates to verify various parts of these stories.
6. Some of the material in this section also appeared in M.M. Lombardo and M.W. McCall, Jr., *Coping with an Intolerable Boss,* Special Report (Greensboro, N.C.: Center for Creative Leadership, January 1984), and M.M. Lombardo and M.W. McCall, Jr., "The Intolerable Boss," *Psychology Today,* January 1984, 45–48.
7. C. Argyris, "Interpersonal Competence and Organizational Effectiveness"; M.M. Lombardo, *Values in Action: The Meaning of Executive Vignettes,* Technical Report No. 28 (Greensboro, N.C.: Center for Creative Leadership, 1986).
8. M.M. Lombardo, *Values in Action.*

Chapter 4. Hardships

1. Though little research has dealt directly with the developmental potential of hardships, there have been studies whose conclusions, taken as a whole, support this generalization. These include Glickman et al., *Top Management Development and Succession;* Kaplan et al., *High Hurdles: The Challenge of Executive Self-development;* Kobasa, "Stressful Life Events, Personality, and Health: An Inquiry into Hardiness"; Sheehy, *Pathfinders;* Vaillant, *Adaptation to Life;* and Zaleznik, "Management of Disappointment."
2. See, for example, M.M. Lombardo and M.W. McCall, Jr., *Coping with an Intolerable Boss.*
3. The authors don't know for sure if this saying was original with the executive. Our efforts to identify another source failed to turn one up.

Chapter 5. Making the Most of Experience

1. C. Yeager and L. Janos, *Yeager: An Autobiography* (New York: Bantam, 1985), 134.
2. T. Wolfe, *The Right Stuff* (New York: Bantam, 1980).
3. C. Yeager and L. Janos, *Yeager: An Autobiography,* 319.
4. Ibid., 83–84.
5. Ibid., 1.
6. F.E. Fiedler, "Leadership Experience and Leader Performance," *Organizational Behavior and Human Performance* 5 (1970):1–14.
7. For a detailed discussion of the elements in each kind of experience, see Lindsey et al., *Key Events in Executives' Lives.*
8. See, for example, M.W. McCall, Jr., and C.A. McCauley, "Analyzing the Developmental Potential of Jobs." In J.L. Moses (Chair), *Expanded Potential for Job Analysis,* Symposium conducted at the meeting of the American Psychological Association, Washington, D.C., August 1986.
9. See the appropriate chapters in Lindsey et al., *Key Events in Executives' Lives.*
10. Lombardo and McCall, *Coping with an Intolerable Boss.*
11. J.J. Gabarro, *The Dynamics of Taking Charge* (Boston, Mass.: Harvard Business School Press, 1987). Also M.W. McCall, Jr., and M.L. Lombardo, *Off the Track: Why and How Successful Executives Get Derailed,* Technical Report No. 21 (Greensboro, N.C.: Center for Creative Leadership, January 1983).
12. Kotter, *The General Managers.*
13. V.J. Bentz, *Explorations of Scope and Scale: The Critical Determinant of High Level Executive Effectiveness,* Technical Report No. 31 (Greensboro, N.C.: Center for Creative Leadership, September 1987).
14. Kotter, *The General Managers,* 135.
15. W. Bennis and B. Nanus, *Leaders: The Strategies for Taking Charge* (New York: Harper and Row, 1985), 188–189.
16. R. Heinlein, *Time for the Stars* (New York: Ballantine, 1978), 99.
17. W. Bennis and B. Nanus, *Leaders: The Strategies for Taking Charge,* 57–58.
18. T.J. Peters and R.H. Waterman, Jr., *In Search of Excellence: Lessons From America's Best-Run Companies* (New York: Harper and Row, 1982).
19. Also a major finding reported in W. Bennis and B. Nanus, *Leaders: The Strategies for Taking Charge.*
20. See also J.J. Gabarro, *The Dynamics of Taking Charge,* and M.W. McCall, Jr., and M.M. Lombardo, *Off the Track.*
21. J. Bronowski, *The Ascent of Man* (Boston, Mass.: Little, Brown, 1973), 115–116.
22. W. Manchester, *American Caesar: Douglas MacArthur* (New York: Dell, 1978), 15.
23. T. Wolfe, *The Right Stuff,* 19.

Chapter 6. Making It Work: The Corporate Opportunity

1. T.J. Peters and R.H. Waterman, Jr., *In Search of Excellence.*
2. See J.P. Kotter, "General Managers Are Not Generalists," *Organizational Dynamics* (Spring 1982):4–19, and Y.K. Shetty and N.S. Perry, Jr., "Are Top Executives Transferable Across Companies?" *Business Horizons* (June 1976):23–28.
3. Kotter, *The Leadership Factor.*
4. McCall and Lombardo, *Off the Track.*
5. Kotter, *The Leadership Factor.*
6. A.E. Pearson, "Muscle-building the Organization," *Harvard Business Review* (July–August 1987):49–55.
7. For a catalog of what has been studied, see Bass, *Stogdill's Handbook of Leadership.*
8. Klimoski and Brickner, "Why Do Assessment Centers Work?"
9. V.J. Bentz, "Research Findings From Personality Assessment of Executives," Paper presented at the Annual Convention of the American Psychological Association, Toronto, Canada (August, 1984).
10. For examples of this procedure, see M. Sorcher, *Predicting Executive Success: What It Takes to Make It into Senior Management* (New York: Wiley, 1985).
11. McCall and Lombardo, *Off the Track.*
12. For alternative sets of criteria, see Bennis and Nanus, *Leaders: The Strategies for Taking Charge;* Kotter, *The General Managers;* T. Peters, *Thriving on Chaos* (New York: Knopf, 1987); and N. Tichy and M.A. Devanna, *The Transformational Leader* (New York: Wiley, 1986).
13. Kotter, *The Leadership Factor,* found this to be true of better-managed companies.
14. Gabarro, *The Dynamics of Taking Charge.*
15. Kotter, *The General Managers;* Gabarro, *The Dynamics of Taking Charge.*
16. More detail on courses can be found in Lindsey et al., *Key Events in Executives' Lives,* 177–189.
17. L. Thomas, *The Medusa and the Snail* (New York: Viking, 1979), 28.
18. The charts in this book and the additional descriptive material in Lindsey et al., *Key Events in Executives' Lives* can provide a starting point.
19. Kotter, *The General Managers.*

References

Allen, Frank. "Bosses List Main Strengths, Flaws Determining Potential of Managers." *Wall Street Journal,* November 14, 1980.

Argyris, Chris. "Interpersonal Competence and Organizational Effectiveness." In *Interpersonal Dynamics,* edited by W.G. Bennis, E.H. Schein, D.E. Berlew, and G.I. Steel. Homewood, Ill.: Dorsey, 1968.

Bass, Bernard M., ed. *Stogdill's Handbook of Leadership.* New York: Free Press, 1981.

Bennis, Warren, and Burt Nanus. *Leaders: The Strategies for Taking Charge.* New York: Harper and Row, 1985.

Bentz, V. Jon. *Explorations of Scope and Scale: The Critical Determinant of High Level Executive Effectiveness* (Technical Report No. 31). Greensboro, N.C.: Center for Creative Leadership, September 1987.

Bentz, V. Jon. "Research Findings from Personality Assessment of Executives." Paper presented at the annual convention of the American Psychological Association, Toronto, Canada, August 1984.

Bloom, Benjamin S. "Generalizations About Talent Development." In *Developing Talent in Young People,* edited by Benjamin S. Bloom, 507–549. New York: Ballantine, 1985.

Bray, D.W., R.J. Campbell, and D.L. Grant. *Formative Years in Business: A Long-Term AT&T Study of Managerial Lives.* New York: Wiley, 1974.

Bray, Douglas W., and Ann Howard. "Career Success and Life Satisfactions of Middle-aged Managers." In *Competence and Coping During Adulthood,* edited by L.A. Bond and J.C. Rosen. Hanover, N.H.: University Press of New England, 1980.

Bronowski, Joseph. *The Ascent of Man.* Boston, Mass.: Little, Brown, 1973.

Campbell, John P., Marvin D. Dunnette, Edward E. Lawler III, and Karl E. Weick, Jr. *Managerial Behavior, Performance, and Effectiveness.* New York: McGraw–Hill, 1970.

Dowling, William F. "Conversation: An Interview With Fletcher Byrom." *Organizational Dynamics* 7 (1978):37–60.

Gabarro, John J. *The Dynamics of Taking Charge.* Boston, Mass.: Harvard Business School Press, 1987.

Glickman, A.S., C.P. Hahn, E.A. Fleishman, and B. Baxter. *Top Management Development and Succession.* New York: Committee for Economic Development, 1968.

Grey, R.J., and G.G. Gordon. "Risk-Taking Managers: Who Gets the Top Jobs?" *Management Review* 67 (1978):8–13.

Hall, Douglas T. *Careers in Organizations.* Pacific Palisades, Calif.: Goodyear Publishing Company, 1976.

Hambrick, Donald C. "Environment, Strategy and Power within Top Management Teams." *Administrative Science Quarterly* 26 (1981):253–275.

Heinlein, Robert A. *Time for the Stars.* New York: Ballantine, 1978.

Jennings, George. *The Mobile Manager.* New York: McGraw-Hill, 1971.

Kaplan, Robert E., Wilfred H. Drath, and Joan R. Kofodimos. *High Hurdles: The Challenge of Executive Self-Development* (Technical Report No. 25). Greensboro, N.C.: Center for Creative Leadership, 1985.

Klimoski, Richard, and Mary Brickner. "Why Do Assessment Centers Work? The Puzzle of Assessment Center Validity." *Personnel Psychology* 40 (1987):243–260.

Kobasa, S.C. "Stressful Life Events, Personality, and Health: An Inquiry into Hardiness." *Journal of Personality and Social Psychology,* 37 (1979):1–11.

Kotter, John P. *The General Managers.* New York: Free Press, 1982.

———. "General Managers Are Not Generalists." *Organizational Dynamics* (Spring 1982):4–19.

———. *The Leadership Factor.* New York: Free Press, 1988.

Lindsey, Esther, Virginia Homes, and Morgan W. McCall, Jr. *Key Events in Executives' Lives* (Technical Report No. 32). Greensboro, N.C.: Center for Creative Leadership, 1987.

Lombardo, Michael M. *Values in Action: The Meaning of Executive Vignettes* (Technical Report No. 28). Greensboro, N.C.: Center for Creative Leadership, 1986.

Lombardo, Michael M., and Morgan W. McCall, Jr. *Coping with an Intolerable Boss* (Special Report). Greensboro, N.C.: Center for Creative Leadership, 1984.

Lombardo, Michael M., and Morgan W. McCall, Jr. "The Intolerable Boss." *Psychology Today,* January, 1984, 45–48.

Lombardo, Michael M., and Morgan W. McCall, Jr. "Great Truths That May Not Be." *Issues and Observations,* February 1983, 1–4.

MacKinnon, D.W. "The Assessment and Development of Managerial Creativity." Invited address, Third International Congress on Assessment Center Method, Quebec City, Quebec, Canada, May 28–30, 1975.

Manchester, William. *American Caesar: Douglas MacArthur 1880–1964.* New York: Dell, 1978.

Margerison, C., and A. Kakabadse. *How American Chief Executives Succeed.* New York: American Management Association, 1984.

McCall, Morgan W., Jr., and Michael M. Lombardo. *Off the Track: Why and How Successful Executives Get Derailed* (Technical Report No. 21). Greensboro, N.C.: Center for Creative Leadership, 1983.

McCall, Morgan W., Jr., and Michael M. Lombardo. "What Makes a Top Executive?" *Psychology Today,* February 1983, 26–31.

McCall, Morgan W., Jr., and C.D. McCauley, "Analyzing the Developmental Potential of Jobs." In J.L. Moses (Chair), *Expanded Potential for Job Analysis.* Symposium conducted at the meeting of the American Psychological Association, Washington, D.C., August 1986.

McCall, Morgan W., Jr., Ann M. Morrison, and Robert L. Hannan. *Studies of Managerial Work: Results and Methods* (Technical Report No. 9). Greensboro, N.C.: Center for Creative Leadership, 1978.

McCauley, Cynthia D. *Developmental Experiences in Managerial Work: A Literature Review* (Technical Report No. 26). Greensboro, N.C.: Center for Creative Leadership, 1986.

Mintzberg, Henry. *The Nature of Managerial Work.* New York: Harper and Row, 1973.

Pearson, Andrall E. "Muscle-Build the Organization." *Harvard Business Review,* July–August 1987, 49–55.

Peters, Thomas. *Thriving on Chaos.* New York: Knopf, 1987.

Peters, Thomas J., and Robert H. Waterman, Jr. *In Search of Excellence: Lessons From America's Best-Run Companies.* New York: Harper and Row, 1982.

Sayles, Leonard. *Leadership: What Effective Managers Really Do . . . and How They Do It.* New York: McGraw–Hill, 1979.

Schein, Edgar. *Career Dynamics: Matching Individual and Organizational Needs.* Reading, Mass.: Addison–Wesley, 1978.

Sheehy, G. *Pathfinders.* New York: William Morrow, 1981.

Shetty, Y.K., and N.S. Perry, Jr. "Are Top Executives Transferable Across Companies?" *Business Horizons,* June 1976:23–28.

Short, Alice. "The Corporate Classroom: Are We Getting Our Money's Worth?" *New Management* 4 (Winter 1987): 22–26.

Skinner, Wickham, and Earl Sasser. *Manufacturing in the Corporate Strategy.* New York: Wiley, 1978.

Sonnenfeld, Jeffrey, and John P. Kotter. "The Maturation of Career Theory." *Human Relations* 35 (1982):19–46.

Sorcher, Melvin. *Predicting Executive Success: What It Takes to Make It into Senior Management.* New York: Wiley, 1985.

Stoner, J.A.F., T.P. Ference, E.K. Warren, and H.K. Christensen. *Managerial Career Plateaus.* New York: Center for Research in Career Development, Columbia University, 1980.

Thomas, Lewis. *Late Night Thoughts on Listening to Mahler's Ninth Symphony.* New York: Viking, 1983.

———. *The Medusa and the Snail.* New York: Viking, 1979.

Tichy, Noel, and Mary Anne Devanna. *The Transformational Leader.* New York: Wiley, 1986.

Vaillant, George E. *Adaptation to Life.* Boston, Mass.: Little, Brown, 1977.

Wolfe, Tom. *The Right Stuff.* New York: Bantam, 1980.

Yeager, Chuck, and Leo Janos. *Yeager: An Autobiography.* New York: Bantam, 1985.

Zaleznik, Abraham. "Management of Disappointment." In *Executive Success: Making It in Management,* edited by E.G.C. Collins, 226–244. New York: Wiley, 1983.

Index

Adverse business conditions: developmental potential of, 128–129
Adversity. *See* Hardships
Agendas, 8
Allen, Frank, 16
Ambiguity: learning to cope with, 38–39
American Management Association, 19
Assessment centers, 3, 164–165
AT&T, 16, 19–20
Authority: in fix-it/turnaround assignments, 47–48, 49; in line versus staff assignments, 42; in project assignments, 35

Balance: in the lessons learned, 143–145; between life and work, 93–94
Bennis, Warren, 132, 137
Bosses: bad, 69, 70, 71, 76–79, 125, 179; diversity in exposure to, 12, 73, 81–83, 125, 179; flawed, 69, 70–71, 80–81; good, 69–70, 71, 74–76, 125; lessons from, 68, 69–85, 124–125, 134, 145; role of, in development, 178–180
Bray, Douglas W., 16, 19–20
Breadth versus depth, 170–171
Bronowski, Joseph, 143
Business mistakes, 88, 106–111; lessons from, 112–113
Business schools. *See* Colleges and universities

Career pathing, 158
Career setbacks, 88, 96–100; lessons from, 100–101
Changes, sudden and/or big. *See* Stark transitions

Changing jobs, 88, 102–105; lessons from, 105–106; motives for, 131–132. *See also* Stark transitions
Children. *See* Personal trauma
Classroom. *See* Coursework
Clawson, J. G., 73
Coaching. *See* Mentoring
Colleges and universities: as poor preparation for the realities of work, 19, 22. *See also* Coursework
Committee review (for assessing potential), 165
Confidence. *See* Self-confidence
Corporate identity, 148, 149–151, 159
Corporate strategies and culture: in conglomerates, 149, 151; learning to understand, 39–40. *See also* Management development: and supportive corporate culture
Counseling, hardship or derailment, 177–178
Coursework, 180–183
Crises, 16, 137. *See also* Hardships
Culture, corporate. *See* Corporate strategies and culture

Deficiencies. *See* Weaknesses
Demotion, 187. *See also* Career setbacks; Stark transitions
Derailment. *See* Failure
Derailment factors, 166, 168–169, 181
Development systems. *See* Management development
Developmental assignments, 15–65; core elements, 18, 58–60, 124; identifying, 158, 161–163; learning from, 60–63, 87, 133, 145; potential downsides, 64. *See also* Early work experience;

Developmental assignments (cont.)
 First supervisory experience; Fix-it/
 turnaround assignments; Line-to-staff
 switches; Project/task force assignments; Scope changes; Start-up assignments
Developmental potential of assignments:
 dimensions for assessing, 124–131
Developmental risks: taken by corporations, 151–154, 159
Disadvantages: and developmental potential, 129–130
Diversity of experience, 143, 145, 158,
 186. See also Bosses: diversity in exposure to
Divorce. See Personal trauma
Dowling, William F., 19

Early work experience: and executive development, 17, 18–19, 20–24, 29; lessons from, 25–26. See also First supervisory experience
Engineers: and first supervisory positions, 28
Erroneous learning: from assignments, 133, from hardships, 135; from other people, 134
Executive development. See Management development
Executives, role of, 40, 54–55

Failure, 16, 71, 80–81, 82–83, 142, 177, 187. See also Derailment factors; Hardships
Family life. See Personal trauma
Feedback: accepting when critical, 73; in coursework, 181; on development progress, 11, 12–13; by a first-time supervisor, 28; on how one is perceived, 85, provided by the organization, 155, 177–178, 187; and self-image, 136–137
Firing, 16, 48, 49, 50. See also Career setbacks; Subordinate performance problems
First jobs. See Early work experience
First supervisory experience: and executive development, 17, 19–20, 26–29, 174–175; lessons from, 30–31
Fix-it/turn-around assignments: descriptions of, 18, 45, 47–48, 50–51; lessons from, 9, 11, 48–50, 52–53, 87
Flaws. See Weaknesses

Foreign assignments: contextual factors, 128–129; and disadvantages, 130; and flawed bosses, 80; and start-ups, 15, 43–44; and stigmas, 44

Gabarro, John J., 176, 177
General managers: developmental factors, 3–5
Gordon, G. G., 16
Grey, R. J., 16

Hambrick, Donald C., 16
Hardships, 87–120; learning from, 117–120, 134–135, 145. See also Business mistakes; Career setbacks; Changing jobs; Personal trauma; Subordinate performance problems
High potential. See Talent pool
High-stakes situations: developmental potential of, 127–128
Home. See Personal trauma
Homes, Virginia, 7, 10, 26, 30–31, 36–37, 40–41, 46–47, 52–53, 56–57, 84–85, 94–95, 100–101, 105–106, 112–113, 115–116, 118–119
Howard, Ann, 19–20

Illness. See Personal trauma
Insight, personal, 9; from career setbacks, 96–97, 99–100; from early work experience, 23–24; from hardships, 117, 119–120; from personal trauma, 90–94
Interpersonal skills. See People, dealing with

Jennings, George, 16
Job challenge, 16–17. See also Developmental assignments; Opportunities for growth
Job rotation, 12, 58, 149, 158, 170–171

Kakabadse, Andrew, 19
Kotter, John P., 3, 4, 5, 8, 11, 16, 17, 64, 132, 153, 177, 186

Leadership potential. See Talent pool
Levinson, Daniel J., 68
Lindsey, Esther, 7, 10, 26, 30–31, 36–37, 40–41, 46–47, 52–53, 56–57, 84–85,

Index

94–95, 100–101, 105–106, 112–113, 115–116, 118–119
Line assignments, 42–43, 55, 57. *See also* Fix-it/turnaround assignments; Scope changes; Start-up assignments
Line-to-staff switches: descriptions of, 17, 31–32, 35, 37–38; lessons from, 38–42, 87
Lombardo, Michael M., 168–169

MacArthur, Douglas, 143–144
McCall, Morgan W., Jr., 7, 10, 26, 30–31, 36–37, 40–51, 46–47, 52–53, 56–57, 84–85, 94–95, 100–101, 105–106, 112–113, 115–116, 118–119, 168–169
McCauley, Cynthia D., 2
McGregor, Douglas, 69
MacKinnon, D. W., 16
Management development: characteristics of an effective system, 184–188; and conglomerates, 149–151, 156; corporate investment in, 1–2, 152–154, 159; defined, 147–148; versus selection, 151, 152, 154, 167; and supportive corporate culture, 148, 154–156, 159, 160, 172
Manchester, William, 143–144
Margerison, Charles, 19
Marshall, J., 72
Meaning: searching for, 132–136
Mentoring, 11, 12, 68, 81, 83, 132, 158, 179
Mergers, 97–99
Myths. *See* Stories and myths, organizational

Nanus, Burt, 132, 137

Opportunities for growth: and career threats, 142–143; creating one's own, 100, 122, 131; dimensions for assessing, 124–131, provided by the corporation, 155, 156, 161, 184–185, 186–188; seeking out, 122, 140; taking advantage of, 123–124; viewing flaws as, 137

Peers, dealing with: and business mistakes, 107; learning from, 68
People, dealing with, 19, 31, 34–35, 92, 145; and business mistakes, 107; in fix-it/turnaround assignments, 47–50; and hardships, 119; lessons from 8, 20, 21, 22–23, 67–85, 126–127, 132, 133, 134, 136. *See also* Bosses; Peers; Subordinates
Personal trauma, 88, 89–94; lessons from, 92–95
Persuasion: in fix-it/turnaround assignments, 48–49; in staff assignments, 42
Peters, Thomas J., 149
Politics: and business mistakes, 108, 109; and career setbacks, 97–99; learned from bosses, 83, 145; understanding, 133
Project/task force assignments: descriptions of, 17, 32; lessons from, 31, 32–35, 36–37, 87, 126
Promotions, 96–97, 130, 131–132. *See also* Scope changes

Relationships. *See* People, dealing with
Responsibility: in high-stakes situations, 128; in line versus staff assignments, 42; for management development, 172–174; for one's own development, 73, 138, 186. *See also* Scope changes
"Right stuff," 121–122, 146
Risks, 16, 40, 45, 109–110, 127, 140. *See also* Developmental risks
Role models, 69, 134. *See also* Bosses; Mentoring

Sasser, Earl, 16
Schein, Edgar, 16, 19
Scope and scale: developmental potential of, 129
Scope changes: descriptions of, 18, 51; lessons from, 51, 53–55, 56–57, 87, 129; organizational help with, 177
Self-awareness. *See* Insight, personal
Self-confidence: from early work experiences, 23–24; from prior success, 137, 145; from project assignments, 35; from the classroom, 12, 181; from start-up assignments, 45
Self-image, 136–137
Serendipity, 104–105, 184–185
Setbacks. *See* Career setbacks
Shortcomings. *See* Weaknesses
Skinner, Wickham, 16
Staff assignments. *See* Line-to-staff switches
Stakes. *See* High-stakes situations

Stark transitions: developmental potential of, 130–131
Start-up assignments: descriptions of, 17–18, 43–44; lessons from, 9, 15, 43–44, 45, 46–47, 87
Stewart, R., 72
Stories and myths, organizational: and business mistakes, 109–110
Strategies, corporate. *See* Corporate strategies and culture
Stress, 16, 127
Subordinate performance problems, 47–48, 88, 111, 113–115, 117; lessons from, 115–116, 125–126; and procrastination, 113, 114
Subordinates, dealing with: and business mistakes, 107; in first supervisory jobs, 26–29; and developing, in scope changes, 53–54; learning from, 68, 125–126. *See also* Subordinate performance problems
Succession planning, 165, 167
Supportive cultures. *See* Management development: and supportive corporate culture

Talent pool: advantages/disadvantages of, 160; creating, 163–167, 170; identifying, 156–157
Task force. *See* Project/task force assignments
Temperament: of executives, 8–9, 48–50
Thomas, Lewis, 184

Threatening situations: anticipating, 142–143
Timing: of formal coursework, 180, 181; of interventions and job changes, 104, 175–176; of training experiences, 12
Training programs, 11, 12. *See also* Coursework
Turn-arounds. *See* Fix-it/turn-around assignments
Twain, Mark, 64

Uncertainty, 16, 38–39, 102, 140
Unions, dealing with, 74, 75, 126
Universities. *See* Colleges and universities

Values: basic, 8; bosses as sources of, 73, 75, 76, 78, 79, 82, 83, 179; and vicarious lessons, 88; warped, 134

Waterman, Robert H., Jr., 149
Weaknesses (one's own): accepting responsibility for, 137–138, 139; balanced with strengths, 144; compensating for, 137, 139, 140–142; correcting, 138, 139, 141, 142; and organizational counseling, 177–178; recognizing, 96, 110–111, 117, 119–120, 136, 137, 139, 140. *See also* Derailment factors
Wives. *See* Personal trauma
Wolfe, Tom, 121

Yeager, Chuck, 121–123

About the Authors

Morgan W. McCall, Jr., has spent his career studying managers and executives and developing applications of that knowledge. Articles based on his research have appeared in such diverse outlets as *The Academy of Management Journal, The Journal of Occupational Psychology, Management Science, Psychology Today, The New York Times,* Center for Creative Leadership technical and special reports, and several textbooks. In addition he has coauthored four other books: *Leadership: Where Else Can We Go?* (Duke Press), *Whatever It Takes: Decision Makers at Work* (Prentice Hall), *Looking Glass: An Organizational Simulation* (Scott Foresman), and *Key Events in Executives' Lives* (Center for Creative Leadership). Applying his work has involved him in management and executive education, consultation with a number of major corporations, and frequent appearances on the lecture circuit. Dr. McCall has been a senior behavioral scientist at the Center for Creative Leadership; currently he is a senior research scientist in the Center for Effective Organizations as well as visiting professor in the School of Business Administration at the University of Southern California in Los Angeles. A fellow of the American Psychological Association, he has a B.S. from Yale and a Ph.D. from Cornell.

Michael M. Lombardo is director, Leadership Development Research Group at the Center for Creative Leadership. He has done research on executive progress and development and is coauthor of a psychological instrument which measures how well a manager learns the lessons needed for success. Other publications he has authored or coauthored on executive development include *Values in Action: The Meaning of Executive Vignettes* (Center for Creative Leadership, 1986), "How Do Leaders Get To Lead?" (*Issues & Observations,* February 1982), and "Great Truths That May Not Be . . . Management Homilies: Do They Stand Up Under Examination?" (*Management Review,* 1983). He is lead author of *Looking Glass: An Organizational Simulation* (CCL); coauthor with Morgan W. McCall, Jr., of *Leadership: Where Else Can We Go?;* and author of numerous articles and technical reports. Mike also heads a research effort on managerial effectiveness and consults regularly with a number of major corporations. He holds a B.A. from the University of North Carolina, Chapel Hill, and an M.A. and Ed.D. from the University of North Carolina, Greensboro.

Ann M. Morrison, director for the San Diego office of the Center for Creative Leadership (CCL), has been with that organization at its Greensboro, N.C., headquarters for thirteen years. During that time she has conducted research and executive training programs for such companies as Eastman Kodak, General Electric, IBM, and Westinghouse Electric as well as numerous other organizations in the private and public sectors. Immediately prior to opening CCL–San Diego, Morrison served as division director of the center, managing a worldwide network of organizations licensed to conduct the center's programs. She is the author of several books and papers on leadership development. Her latest book was *Breaking the Glass Ceiling: Can Women Reach the Top of America's Largest Corporations?,* targeted to aspiring women managers and professionals.

A researcher with extensive training in how executives learn how to handle the demands of top jobs, Morrison played an important role in the Greensboro community. She is a graduate of Leadership Greensboro, was the president of the Women's Professional Forum there, and served on the Greensboro Chamber of Commerce's Council on Economic Development.

A native of Easton, Penn., Morrison holds a master's degree in psychology from Bucknell University in Pennsylvania, and an M.B.A. from Wake Forest University in North Carolina.